Surfing Long Beach Island

Caroline Unger

Copyright © 2003 by Caroline Unger.

ISBN :   Hardcover   1-4134-0809-5
             Softcover   1-4134-0808-7

All rights reserved. No part of this book may be reproduced or transmitted in any form or by any means, electronic or mechanical, including photocopying, recording, or by any information storage and retrieval system, without permission in writing from the copyright owner.

This book was printed in the United States of America.

To order additional copies of this book, contact:
Xlibris Corporation
1-888-795-4274
www.Xlibris.com
Orders@Xlibris.com

Surfing
Long Beach Island

Contents

Forward 7
Introduction to Long Beach Island 13
The Long Beach Island Surfer 16
The First Wave 22
      Henry "Stretch" Pohl (1911-1983)
      William "Wimpy" Paulsworth (1939-1983)
      Charles "Chill" Paul
      Carl "Tinker" West
The First Surf Shops 39
    SURF SHOP PHENOMENON
    RON JON SURF SHOP
      Reverend Earl Comfort
      John Spodofora
    KOFEFF'S SURF SHOP
      Dean Ward
      Baugh Brothers
      Roger Bakst
      Bruce "Huckleberry" Saunders
      Dick Crosta
    WALTERS SURF SHOP
      Bobby Jensen
    ACUFF SURF SHOP
    BRANT BEACH SURF SHOP—Richard Lisiewski
    RICK SURF SHOP—Jim Fitz-Randolph
    CHITO'S SURF SHOP
Sixties Long Beach Island Surfing Contests 85

Ladies of Long Beach Island 89
      Barbara (Oughton) Baptista, a.k.a. "Barb"
      Patrica Browning (Lauer) Roth, a.k.a.
      "Bonnie" or "Hazel Hotcurl"

        Mary (Buck) Frack
        Barbara Conover
        Barbara Robertson a.k.a. "Magnolia Bulkhead"
Local Surf Legends 98
        Chuck Barfoot
        Ken Smith
        Tom Luker
        Surfing Swami
        Poling Productions
        Rocket Power
        Jason Murray
        Bilderback's Lens
        Chris Pfeil
        Return of the Wooden Surfboard
        Joe's Smile
Southern Regional High School Surfing Team 132
        Noel Huelsenbeck
        Tom Ackers
        Justin Citta
        Sammy Zuegner
        Ben McBrien
        Randy Townsend
        Jamie DeWitt
        Brendan Willem
Holyoke Avenue Surfers Alliance 142
New Jersey Surf Club 147
Local Boards 149
        Pohl
        Collier/Matador
        Holden
        Planet Blue
        Kretzer
        Line Drive
        Boardman
Local Breaks 163
Surfing the Web 170
Why We Surf 175
Acknowledgements 201

Forward

This book is written for every Long Beach Island surfer who has ever had to answer the question, often spoken with a condescending inflection, "You mean there's surf in New Jersey?" Not only is there surf, brudda but I'll be so bold as to say that our little island has influenced surfing history.

Several LBI natives have achieved national status in the amateur and professional surfing ranks. Others have surfed throughout the world, holding their own in "expert" conditions. More than a few locals have tried their hand at surfboard design and manufacturing. LBI was the birthplace of a retail giant that is known throughout the international surfing industry. From cartoons to photography, movie production and offshoots of the sport like snowboarding, LBI'ers have been making their mark on surfing culture since the 1930s, and are still going strong.

The names in this book have not been changed to protect the innocent. These are hard-core surfers, individuals whose commitment to surfing is a lifestyle, not just a hobby. I can vouch for that, because I had to find them in order to write their stories. I was often delayed because of their surfing commitments. Chuck Barfoot was away surfing in Brazil and Bill Kretzer was in Puerto Rico. Jamie DeWitt was competing in surf meets in North Carolina and Bob Nugent was working a hundred hours a week in the summer to support his surfing habit.

So, what makes a soul surfer? There is a lifelong quest to pursue happiness, in one of its purest forms. There is less encumbrance to the material world and a heightened awareness of the need for preservation of our natural resources. Surfers, regardless of age, possess the energy and antics of youth. There is a drive for adventure and the desire to travel, travel, travel, in the pursuit of waves. These characteristics often make it necessary to adopt different work principles from mainstream society. Regardless of which era the surfer is from, what walk of life or educational background, you will see that these are common threads that connect the surfing community.

This quest to enjoy life, through the medium of the ocean, has resulted in some bad press from the "real world." The surfer is often ridiculed as having a poor work ethic or being a "beach bum." Even Bear, in the classic surfing movie *Big Wednesday*, observed "That's what I get for hiring surfer labor."

During an interview for the surfing documentary *Liquid Stage: The Lure of Surfing*, Steve Pezman, publisher of *The Surfers Journal*, explained why he thought surfers of his generation were labeled as rebels:

> *Against the larger societal push for conformity which characterized the 1950s, surfers' priority of riding waves was not warmly embraced by mainstream society. They were viewed as rebels. For surfers of the late 1950s, their parents were children of the depression. Like my father, they were conditioned to get a job and keep it at all cost. Life was about being white-knuckled to an income. As a surfer, those rules and paranoia were not worth worshipping for the rest of our lives.*

Surfers don't necessarily work less, just differently. Do you want to tell surfers who are seasonal business owners, that they lack a work ethic? They work seven days a week with fifteen hour days. In doing this, they put themselves in a position to take time off later, to enjoy their favorite winter surfing spots. It is really all a matter of priorities. Surfers, somehow, some way, find a way to fit their work around their passion.

The surfing culture on LBI in the 1950s and 1960s was closely connected to the clamming industry. Many a surfer spent his time treading for clams in the bay. It was an appealing job since there wasn't a nine to five schedule that conflicted with the most opportune surfing conditions. Those who needed more money just stayed out in the bay a little longer. In those days, the bay was bountiful and the pay was good. Many a surfer worked his way through college working in the bay. Commercial clamming is still a source of livelihood for surfers like Chill Paul, Bill Willem, and Bonnie Roth.

In recent years, with the boom in property values in Ocean County, many surfers have found a way to make a comfortable living around their surfing schedules while working in various aspects of construction or real estate. Sure, surfers can be doctors and lawyers, too, but a good day of golf still can't compete with a good day of surfing.

Surfers have always had a strong connection to the environment and a commitment to its preservation. You will find that most surfers engage in environmentally-conscious activities. After all, when something is wrong with the ocean, surfers are often the first to know. Paddling above and through the waves, sometimes hours at a time, every sense is aroused. The surfer **tastes** the water, **smells** it, **hears** the thundering inside break. When he **sees** the spray from an off-shore wind, he knows that catching the wave will be just a little more work. The surfer submerges his whole body and **feels** the ocean's invigorating briskness. When the ocean is sick, the surfer feels sick.

Some people experience heightened spirituality through their surfing. Sitting out on the water inevitably arouses a sense of awe for the natural environment. Being able to see and experience the world's oceans becomes more important than amassing worldly possessions. The finest hotels and five-star restaurants are a distant second to being able to live in primitive accommodations in a third-world country if there is surf to be had.

Surfers have been known to sacrifice financial security to maintain their surfing lifestyles. Mickey Munoz, in an interview for the *Today Show*, was asked: "For fifty-four years you've devoted yourself to this (surfing) . . . Why?" Mickey, as you may recall, was the body-double for Sandra Dee's surfing scenes during the 1959 movie, *Gidget*. He was also a pioneer big wave rider, who, along with Greg Noll, was one of the first to ever successfully surf Waimea Bay. It was pointed out to him that many of his contemporaries were now getting ready to retire on healthy pensions, in big houses and with fancy cars. Without thinking twice, he proudly told the world:

> *When the waves are good, the waves are good. It's such a rare opportunity that I don't want to have to wear a watch, I don't want to have to be anywhere. I love just being in the water and the rhythm. The positives are so positive and the highs are so high . . . they far outweigh the negatives.*

One of the comments I heard repeatedly from those I interviewed was their shared pride and joy to be able to pass on the surfing experience to their children. There was also the thrill of traveling to exotic places with lifelong friends. Unfortunately, there was also an underlying tone of apprehension. Many fear the devastating impact that pollution will have, not only on surfing, but on the environment as a whole.

One of my favorite sections of the book is the "Why We Surf" chapter. For one thing, I didn't have to write anything. It's all unedited material from a wide variety of surfers—all different ages, occupations, and surfing experience, albeit with an LBI connection. Admittedly, I copied the idea from the April '95 edition of *Surfer* magazine, where there were eighty-five reasons from individuals who read like a "Who's Who" in the surfing world. I'd like to think our chapter reads like a "Who's Who on LBI." What I did learn from trying to get the surveys back is that most surfers aren't exactly type-A personalities. When I asked folks to get them back to me in one month, I was pretty lucky to get them back in two. You know who you are out there—now aren't you glad that I nagged you?

My sincere thanks to all of you who so graciously allowed me into your lives. Thank you for the opportunity to enter your homes, your photo albums, and your hearts. For some, I hope these next chapters will bring back many fond memories. I think you will agree that despite all the changes through the years—huge product merchandising, more crowded beaches, new surfboard design and technology—the stoke is still the same. I hope that the next generation of surfers will feel empowered to promote the positive aspects of this incredible sport and lifestyle, and to keep the "aloha spirit" alive. For anyone who is still new to the sport, I offer one additional insight from the character, David, in Disney's animated film *Lilo & Stitch*:

> *I may not be a doctor but I know that there is no better cure for a sour face than a couple boards and some choice waves.*

References:

Big Wednesday. Warner Brothers, Inc., 1978.

Lilo & Stitch, Walt Disney Pictures, 2002.

Liquid Stage: The Lure of Surfing.
    KPBS Television San Diego, 1995.

Today Show, NBC, August 28, 2002.

Introduction to Long Beach Island

The Causeway – Gateway to LBI
Photo: Pfeil

Long Beach Island is an eighteen mile stretch of fine beach sand, shifting sandbars, and man-made wooden and rock jetties. Traveling to this barrier island, one must drive through rich acres of preserved pinelands. It "feels" far away from the two large metropolitan areas that are within driving distance-New York City (90 miles from LBI) and Philadelphia (60 miles from LBI).

Long Beach Island comprises only a small segment of the 130 miles of New Jersey coastline. For all intents and purposes, it is an obscure coastal town. It doesn't have a boardwalk or the "nightlife" that many of its counterparts boast. It certainly doesn't have the glitz and glitter of Atlantic City. Nevertheless, the people who are attracted to LBI are richly rewarded with its natural resources. Even the researchers, like Stephen Leatherman, a.k.a. "Dr. Beach," agree that LBI is something special. LBI has twice been selected as one of the *Top Twenty Beaches in America*. The study conducted by the Laboratory for Coastal Research at Florida International University uses fifty criteria from water quality to sand condition. LBI is the only New Jersey beach to ever make the list.

Most people enjoy LBI between June and September. The year-round population is about 8,000 people. During the summer, that number can swell to 140,000. The island is reached by a two-mile, four-lane causeway which is located at just about the island's mid-section. There are actually six separate towns on LBI, each with their own governing bodies. Moving north to south, the first town is Barnegat Light. Like all good shore communities, LBI does have a lighthouse and conveniently, it is located here. Other towns include: Harvey Cedars, Surf City, Ship Bottom, Beach Haven, and Long Beach Township.

Long Beach Township, the largest municipality on LBI, consists of seven small towns north and south of the Causeway. The twelve-mile township includes North Beach at its northern-most point, but there is also a North Beach Haven south of the Causeway but north of Beach Haven! Add to that, towns like Beach Haven Park, Beach Haven Crest, Beach Haven Gardens, and just for a little diversity, Haven Beach. The names of the towns are important as we talk about some of the different surf breaks. Don't worry if you're confused by all the names - you're not alone. These little subtleties contribute to greater than fifty percent of the nervous breakdowns by postal workers.

People on LBI make their living providing resort-type amenities. Many locals own restaurants, retail businesses, or provide the means for recreational activities (sailing, boating, fishing, crabbing, windsurfing, parasailing, kitesailing, surfing, biking, and putt-putt golf). Folks involved in all phases of construction are also in demand as beach bungalows are being torn down, one-by-one, and replaced with pretentious dwellings. Then there are the realtors, who outnumber year-round residents. Another island industry, although less well-known, is the commercial fishing fleet in Barnegat Light. It is one of the busiest on the eastern seaboard with over five million pounds of seafood shipped every year, to places as distant as Europe and Asia.

LBI is also known for its good surfing conditions, although this is not something the average summer visitor knows. Sure, surfers can be found during the summer months, but usually out of desperation. Except for occasional low pressure systems, the prevailing southerly winds result in waves that have a closer resemblance to boat wakes.

The surfing community has a better understanding of how coastal areas can have seasonal Jekyll and Hyde personalities. On LBI, surfers start thinking about heading out in the water just as normal people start retreating to the warmth and comfort of their homes. The surfer may be pelted by rain, perhaps from the remnants of a hurricane that is headed out to sea. At other times, gusts of wind from a blustery winter nor'easter threaten to snatch the surfboard from one's hands. It doesn't matter. If nature brings surf, the LBI surfers will be there . . . celebrating life the best way that they know how . . . in a harmonious dance with the waves.

The Long Beach Island Surfer

The Long Beach Island surfer must be patient to wait through the sweltering heat and humidity of an East Coast summer. Air temperatures range between 80° to 100° while the water temperature may rise as high as 75°. The typical lull in the waves is really just the gestation period for the beast that is about to come. It's when everyone starts to go home, after Labor Day, that the tropical storms and hurricanes begin to pass offshore. Even a storm that is hundreds of miles away will churn up worthwhile swells.

The crowds have gone . . . Soul surfer and an autumn swell

As the winter solstice approaches, frequent nor'easters become part of the weather pattern. These destructive Atlantic storms have been wreaking havoc on the northeastern seaboard for centuries. Surfers are well-aware of the powerful punch that they pack into the waves. Part of that punch is also the painful temperatures of air and sea. Temperatures are lowest in January and February. Water temperatures have been known to drop below freezing. Add to that, blustery winds that may bring wind chills below zero degrees.

Nevertheless, the hard core East Coast surfer can not pass up these bigger, more consistent waves of winter. Like knights, clad in armor of neoprene from head to toe, they launch their attack. Unlike their medieval counterparts, however, their face is left exposed to the wind and wetness. The beautiful spray from a strong offshore wind adds to the throbbing. The infamous "ice cream headache" is inevitable with too many submersions. The whole "feel" of surfing is just a little different. Is it possible for water to feel harder? All movements are just a little slower with the 5mm outer covering. All sounds are muffled through the hood. People who think you're crazy don't understand that for the most part you're actually pretty warm inside. The coolness that you do feel invigorates you and makes you feel alive through all your senses. It's something you take home with you as you paddle in, and the seal that has been swimming with you wonders why you're leaving.

As the earth begins to thaw in the spring, surfers also slowly shed their coverings. The thickness of the wetsuit can be decreased. More skin is gradually exposed to the elements. The hood comes off first and then the gloves and the boots. By June, the wetsuits with short sleeves and short pants are usually in order. Compared to the mainland, the air temperature will remain cooler on the island in the spring, insulated by the coolness of the bay and ocean waters. An occasional nor'easter will still come through, assailing the buds and flowers as they try to make their debut in yet another change of the seasons.

Few surfers in the world experience the extreme change in air and water temperatures that LBI surfers do. The size and shape of the wave from day to day, and even beach to beach, is also extremely variable. It is obvious that the LBI surfer is very adaptable and very committed.

LBI locals have proven to be skilled enough to handle surf all over the world. When they weren't going out to the world, the world came to them. Several LBI surfers have been forever captured for the world to see in surfing magazines and movies. Local writers and filmmakers have also made their mark. Here are a few examples:

MAGAZINES & BOOKS:

Bakst, Roger. "The Dynamic Duo: Puerto Rico's Crashboat and Gas Chamber" *International Surfing* **1969, 75-77.**

LBI locals, Sam and Ernie Baugh, are mentioned in the article as "some Rincon regulars who rode Crashboat well last winter." The article also features two pictures of Sam Baugh getting in AND out of a sizable tube. Story and photos are by Roger Bakst who also worked and surfed on LBI.

Borte, Jason. "Heat Wave: Sweating Out Hurricane Season Along the East Coast." *Surfer* **43(2), 2001, 76-95.**

This is a thirty-one picture spread that takes you from New Hampshire to South Florida. The teaser on the cover is "THE BEST EAST COAST TUBE EVER SEEN." Turn to page 88 and you'll find John Bilderback's two page picture of Beach Haven local, Sammy Zuegner in that famous Holyoke Avenue tube ride. Bilderback also needed two pages to capture Greg Pobst off the lip of another LBI wave. Photographer Joe Coffey couldn't resist a shot of young Surf City local, Brenden Willem, stylin' at Manasquan. (Brendan reports the shot was really taken on LBI). If you want an ahhh moment, there's even a Beach Haven sunrise in the feature.

DiMenna, Ron. "Atlantic Advice." *Atlantic Surfing* **1(2), 1965, 9.**

Surfing fundamentals for beginners

DiMenna, Ron. "Long Beach Island on the Atlantic." *International Surfing* **June, 1965, 52-55.**
A brief description of LBI with a collection of pictures and some of the early names.

Ker, John. "Beach Haven." *Surfer* **13(6), 1973, 79-83.**
The five lines of text only mention a place "somewhere on the much-lambasted eastern coastline of the United States," but you'll know that it's our island when you see a picture taken at Maryland Avenue and another of Ray DeFrehn. There are nine pictures in all, taken by John Ker and Bruce Ker.

Ker, John. "New Jersey: A Last Look." *Surfer* **14(6), 1974, 48-49.**
There are ten pictures of New Jersey including Arthur Seger riding in Brant Beach and some Beach Haven roof-tops. Also included are shots of Seaside Heights, Bay Head, and Sea Girt. There is a brief text about winter surfing.

Kirk, Cameron & Hanle, Zack. 1968. *The Surfer's Handbook.* **New York City: Dell Publishing.**
This paperback includes information from basic oceanography to surfing techniques. Of special interest is the chapter: "Surfing Spots around the World." Nearly four hundred spots are mentioned and LBI is included! Of the sixteen photographs in the book, three of them are from LBI! Several East Coast pictures were taken by Roger Bakst.

Pfeil, Christopher. "The Quiet Season: Winter Solitude in New Jersey." *The Surfers Journal* **11(4), 2002, 72-81.**
A thirteen picture spread of crisp black and white photos that make you feel like you're looking at works of art. The local surfers featured include: Jeremy Lees, Randy Townsend, Greg Luker, Bob Selfrige, and Chris Kretzler.

Stanford, Ron. "Tom Luker: One-Way Ticket To Paradise."
Surfer 36(6), 1995, 60.
This short article re-caps Tom's LBI connection and how his making of the film, "Atlantic Crossing," led him to discover and eventually move to Puerto Rico.

MOVIES:

Atlantic Crossing. **Tom Luker (1989).**
This film, focusing on the east coast, was the brain child of LBI surfer, Tom Luker. He gets some help from experienced cinematographer, Paul Prewitt. Footage of local talent, Justin Citta and Greg Luker in Peru, Chili, and Brazil. You'll also catch footage of Hawaii, North Carolina, Florida, New Hampshire and an impressive Montauk Point, N.Y. going off at a solid 20 feet.

Drenched In Devotion. **A Garage Conspiracy Production (2001).**
Lifelong LBI surfer and extensive surf traveler, Neil Saunders, stayed right at home to film this one. It's all longboard, all East Coast with insightful interviews from Greg Noll, "Balsa" Bill Yerkes, Tony Caramanico, and even Neil's dad, local legend, Huckleberry.

L.B.I. Saltwater High. **Poling Productions (1989).**
The videocassette was released by: Back to the Shore Video Magazine. The film is loaded with historical LBI footage including: 1949 Lucy Evelyn and 1959 Causeway construction. You'll be able to witness the destruction following Hurricane Carol in 1959 and the Storm of 1962. There is also LBI surfing footage from 1962 through the 1980s including Hurricane Belle of 1976. There is rare footage of surfing legends, Mark Foo, Mike Parsons, and Hans Hederman surfing Harvey Cedars.

***Summer Surfari*. Poling Productions (1985).**
This film premiered at the Long Beach Island Foundation of the Arts and Sciences. Footage includes segments from Barbados, the Caribbean, Hawaii, Indonesia, California, and Florida. A five-minute segment of *Summer Surfer* was even featured on the television program, *Solid Gold*.

***What Exit 2*. What Exit Productions (2002).**
Northeast surfers and skaters are featured, doing their thing from New England to Florida. There is also footage from Barbados and Hawaii. The soundtrack is packed with alternative and punk tunes. You'll find a lot of footage of LBI locals including: Justin Citta, Greg Luker, Ben McBrien, Joe Muzillo, Mike Roth, Brendan Willem, and Sam Zuegner.

The First Wave

WHY DO YOU SURF?

To me, it is a way of life. I can get more relaxation from six rides on a surfboard than some people can get out of a gallon of gin. I like the challenge, the unexpectedness of events, the sound of the wave and exhilaration of beating the wave which tries to destroy you. I'll surf as long as I'm able to walk. Of course, I'm slower and can't get up as fast as I once did, but I know that is all in the game. I know of no sport that gives me as much satisfaction as surfing does.

—Stretch Pohl
from "Stretch Pohl-Surfer,"
The Beachcomber, July 17, 1969

Henry "Stretch" Pohl (1911-1983)

After being sick in bed for over a week, the teenage Henry gradually got his strength back. When he stood up again, it looked as though he had grown a foot. Ever since then, he has been known as "Stretch." He eventually grew into his muscular 6'2" frame, but would become "larger than life" to the New Jersey surfing community, past and present. He will forever be known as a gifted athlete, a skilled waterman, and an individual respected by all. Stretch was a man whose passion for the water brought the sport of surfing to stay on the East Coast. It's not surprising that he earned the title from *Surfing East* magazine: "New Jersey's Duke Kahanamoku."

Stretch was the consummate athlete, participating in varsity football, track, basketball, wrestling, and, of course, swimming. After graduating from the University of Delaware in 1934, he briefly played with a professional football team. He began his teaching career in New Jersey in 1935 at Westmont Public School. He later taught science and coached at Teaneck, Ramapo, and Haddonfield High Schools. He left high school teaching briefly to teach physics at Paterson State Teacher's College. It was at that time that he served as a line coach under the legendary Vince Lombardi at St. Cecilia's High School in Englewood.

A native of Camden, Stretch began visiting LBI in 1928. He lived in northern New Jersey in the winters and eventually built a summer home in Surf City with his wife Irene. Loveladies became his permanent home when he retired.

Stretch surfed for the first time in 1932 on 20th Street in Ship Bottom. Stretch was twenty-one years old, but surfing equipment was only in its infancy. The first hollow surfboard had just been invented in 1928 by Tom Blake in California. Blake's hollow board was a groundbreaking development. It significantly decreased the weight of a surfboard and effectively replaced the solid redwood boards of the early 1900s.

The first board that Stretch owned was a limited production, Blake hollow board. It was 12' long with a pointed tail and rounded nose. The sport of surfing at that time consisted of aiming these large wooden missiles toward the beach and riding them straight in. Stretch's first board pre-dated the use of a fin for steering. Fins were introduced by Tom Blake in 1935.

Stretch was always intimately connected to the water. He taught swimming and water safety to hundreds of people in his lifetime. He served as the National Red Cross Director of Safety in the Paterson area from 1941-1956. In a later position as Water Safety Director for Ocean County, Stretch demonstrated a Blake rescue board to ocean lifeguards. It didn't take long for these lifeguards to realize that the rescue paddleboards could also be used for catching waves. Many lifeguards were introduced to surfing in this way by Stretch. He also made it possible for the average person to learn about surfing through the Stretch Pohl Surfing School he ran in Holgate from 1968 to 1969.

Stretch spent a lifetime studying the sport of surfing and truly made it a way of life. His pursuits to learn about technique and equipment, and then to graciously teach others, popularized the sport more than even he could ever have imagined. He continued to correspond with one of surfing history's greatest individuals, Tom Blake (1902-1994). Stretch also kept in contact with several other Californians involved in the surfing industry. He shared the news of growing West Coast trends with their eager East Coast counterparts. Stretch compiled information in two separate water safety manuals entitled: *Paddleboard Technique* and *Paddleboard Manual*.

The first surfboards that Stretch built were hollow wooden boards. From there, the industry moved to composite boards using woods of different weights. Stretch made his version of a balsa and redwood board (balsa for its lightness and redwood for its stability) just before fiberglass made its debut on the West Coast. Unfortunately, he soon found his beautiful wood craftsmanship outdated in the water. Fortunately, when cut down to a four foot section, one of his boards made an eye-catching breakfast nook that is still in the Pohl home today.

Even though Stretch's surfing roots were deeply embedded in the earliest history of surfing—a day when surfboards weren't much more than heavy wooden planks, he was progressive in his mindset. He enthusiastically watched the sport develop as it moved from fiberglass covered balsa wood to fiberglass covered polyurethane foam. In a 1969 *Beachcomber* interview, Stretch reported, "I just converted to a mini-board and find it out of this world. It is a 7'8", 23" wide board which I made myself. For a 6'2", 195 pounder, it is quite a thrill to master the 'toothpick'."

Stretch's passion for the water was contagious. Through his efforts, a group of watermen started the Malolo-Akula Surfboard Club in the 1930s. It was housed at Wright's Pier at 20th Street in Ship Bottom. Don't look for this pier today - It was destroyed in the hurricane of 1944. Stretch recounted quite a number of individuals who were surfing in the 1930s including: Mike Howes, Charley Lang, Jack Lounsberry, Tony Steele, and Cary Lincoln (*Beachcomber,* 1969).

Malolo-Akula Surfboard Club with Wright's Pier (20th Street, Ship Bottom) in the background. Left to right: Mike Howes, Cary Lincoln, Erle Jackson, Stretch Pohl. Cary and Erle were killed in the line of duty during World War II.

Stretch was a founding member of the Long Beach Island Surfing Association (L.B.I.S.A.) in March of 1964. This association was initially formed to work with municipal officials to set up surfing hours and surfing beaches as well as help address any surfing problems that arose. In an interview given for *Competition Surf* magazine, Stretch said, "The L.B.I.S.A. stands for clean surfing and good sportsmanship. We obey all laws. We are also trying to prove to the public that surfing is not what some people believe it to be. It's a good clean sport for youngsters as well as oldsters. We hope to promote it by the contests." Stretch served as a judge at many of the local surfing events.

With an athletic ability and passion for the ocean that few other men have possessed, Stretch Pohl surfed skillfully into his late 60s. He surfed several times in California and Puerto Rico but never had the opportunity to visit Hawaii with his wife as he had hoped. A true water person, when he wasn't surfing, he was swimming or clamming. He passed away as the summer sun was setting in August, 1983 at the age of seventy-one. His surfing legacy will never be forgotten. "Mahalo," Stretch. That's Hawaiian for "Thank You."

References:

Hannon, John. "Profiles: Henry 'Stretch' Pohl." *Surfing East*, 1965 Summer: 30-31.

King, Kathryn M. "Henry 'Stretch' Pohl." *Tiki Times*, 1990(2): 6-7.

"Judges Stand III." *Competition Surf,* 1966 Spring: 48.

"Stretch Pohl—Surfer." *The Beachcomber*, July 17, 1969: 6 & 60.

CAROLINE UNGER

HOW WE REMEMBER STRETCH POHL:

I knew Stretch back in the 60s. He didn't pull any punches. If some kid got drunk, Stretch would give him the whole lecture about how alcohol is actually a poison (toxin ... in TOXIC ated), and what it does to your body. He used to say clamming was his therapy. This man was a class act and a gentleman all the way.

> —Robert Stanton: SRHS class of '66. He is originally from Ship Bottom and now works as an oceanographer for the U.S. Government in Long Beach, Mississippi. Robert surfs the Gulf Coast, usually in the Alabama area.

I probably first met Stretch in 1962 or 1963. He was always the "old man" in the group, being in his fifties at the time. He was sensitive about his age, but it didn't matter to us. He was in incredible physical condition for any age. He had no problem staying up with the younger guys. Whether we clamming or surfing, he was always the first one there and the last one to go, a credit to his stamina, he was hard as nails. At the same time, he was a kind and sweet man. He kept in touch with me when I went away to college, sending me a letter about once a week. He was extraordinarily loyal to his friends.

He had an acid sense of humor. Once, while surfing together, Stretch noticed a young teenager during what must have been one of his first surf sessions. After falling off the board multiple times and barely being able to paddle, Stretch looked at me and said, "Who's the Hawaiian?"

Stretch was a great role model. He didn't have any tolerance for guys when they were half-loaded. If they came out in the water hung-over he would ride them pretty hard, saying things like: "What's the matter, is your head too big to fit under water? Do you plan on chumming for sharks?"

—Dave Rinear: Drama Professor
living in San Antonio, Texas
Summers on Cedar Bonnet Island
and still clams Barnegat Bay

He was really a class act and a community-minded guy. Beginning in about 1974 he helped with St. Francis Community Center programs like the 18 Mile Run and recreational programs for kids. He also helped organize the "Cross the Bay Paddleboard Race" to give the watermen another activity. The 3.5 mile race took place from about 1976 to 1980. Stretch was always at the finish line to congratulate you. He was a tremendous role model . . . someone who 'walked the walk'."

—Don Myers: Year-round resident of Brant Beach
Long Beach Township Beach Patrol Supervisor

William "Wimpy" Paulsworth (1939-1983)

Wimpy was a Philadelphia native whose parents owned a summer home on Long Beach Island. His introduction to surfing came in 1958 during a trip to California. At that time, he was making his living as a clammer while living in Surf City. Wimpy sold his clams at the "Clam Stand" in front of the Causeway Inn (no longer exists) on Bay Avenue in Manahawkin. Wimpy thought nothing of leaving his post at the stand in order to go surfing. Chill Paul remembers, "He would leave the clams out in front, and also a jar for patrons to leave their money. It worked in those days."

In the 1960s, this stand was a gathering place for young people who were enthralled by Wimpy. They attentively listened to all his surfing stories. Wimpy was one of the first individuals on the island to ever ride a surfboard. He also teamed up with George Timmons to build a few surfboards. Wimpy's knowledge of surfing surpassed that of most people at the time, but it just wasn't in his personality for big business or self-promotion. In fact, he never even wanted to see surfing develop commercially. He predicted that it would only make the beaches too crowded to enjoy the surf.

Fellow surfer and clammer, Chill Paul, also remembers those days before the crowds, when surfing was just becoming known to the outside world. At that time, Chill, who was an integral part of the LBI Surfing Association, was contacted for an interview by the *Philadelphia Inquirer*. The paper sent a reporter and a photographer on what happened to be one of the biggest days that either Chill or Wimpy had ever seen on the island. "It had to be fifteen to twenty foot." Both men looked at each other as if to say, "I don't want to do this," and then headed out. Wimpy made the cover of the *Sunday Magazine*.

Wimpy will also be remembered for his craftsmanship making hatch cover furniture. Wimpy was the first to make tabletops using actual hatch covers from Liberty ships. To these he applied multiple layers of "surfboard" resin for a thick, glossy coat. They became an LBI tradition and a trend that Ron Jon Surf Shop later developed into a large commercial venture.

Wimpy and his wife Charlene (owner of Bee's Knees—a women's clothing store in Manahawkin and LBI in the 70s and 80s) took winter trips to California and Mexico almost every year. Even in Mexico, Charlene remembers that Wimpy drew a crowd. In Salinas Cruz, he was surrounded by a crowd of clapping Mexicans who had never seen the sport before.

Wimpy passed on early in life, but not without leaving a lasting impression on those who knew him.

Goofy footer, "Wimpy" takes off on an LBI face. This shot appeared in *International Surfing* magazine, June 1965.

Charles "Chill" Paul

Chill's roots in Ocean County go back to his great grandfather who made his living clamming in Barnegat Bay. Every generation since has been involved in the clamming business. Many people know Chill as "Blackey's Clams" on Bay Avenue. He originally rented and then purchased this business from the Black family, twenty-five years ago and counting.

Chill's roots in surfing go back to the early 1960s. At that time, he was on active duty with the U.S. Air Force. With time-off on the weekends, Chill often spent that time clamming in the bay. It was there that he first met the legendary Stretch Pohl who was an avid clammer himself. Stretch introduced Chill to surfing and even built him a board.

Chill teamed up with Stretch Pohl, as well as Reverend Earl Comfort, Ron DiMenna, and Ralph Bourgeois, to form the Long Beach Island Surfing Association (L.B.I.S.A), in March of 1964. In an interview for *Competition Surf* magazine, while serving as president of the organization, Chill discussed the group's rapid growth from 46 members in August of 1964 to over 200 members in 1965. "All through the winter we keep up a continuing campaign to provide more surfing beaches on the whole island. This year (1965) we have a beach in every township with the exception of Surf City. They just don't have an open stretch of beach that they can give us full time. But we do have before and after hours surfing there."

When Chill wasn't promoting surfing on LBI, you could find him out in the water. One of Chill's responsibilities was serving as an advisor to the Air National Guard in Pomona. If Chill was caught up with his work, and his commanding officer was away on a training mission, it was a good time for a call to Ron Jon Surf Shop for a surf report. Chill could jump on the Garden State Parkway and be in the water in no time. On days when there wasn't any surf, Chill even put his twenty-four foot clamming garvey to good use wakeboarding in the bay.

Chill can remember driving the length of the island looking for surf. One day, he and another wave rider desperately canvassed the island from Holgate to Barnegat Light. With no promising swells anywhere, there was nothing left to do but walk to the top of the lighthouse. From that vantage, much to their surprise, they finally found what they were looking for on the north jetty. As far as they know, they were the first to paddle across Barnegat Inlet on surfboards. Chill recalls, "We finally paddled north to the jetty even though the tide was pouring out and carrying us east as fast as we could go."

Chill later joined the U.S. Army and would achieve the rank of Chief Warrant Officer before retiring. He is a decorated veteran of the Korean conflict as well as the Vietnam War. He served in the combat zone of Vietnam where, living on the peninsula, he actually had multiple opportunities for surfing. "A buddy of mine brought back a surfboard from Australia when he was there for his R&R." It was one of only two surfboards that Chill knew of in Vietnam when he was stationed there. The other individual was from another post, so he rarely saw him. Chill was usually alone in the water.

(A) Commander, the sign doesn't say anything about surfing. (B) "Charlie don't surf" (*Apocalypse Now*) - but Chill does. (C) A surreal backdrop - War-torn Vietnam (D) The "necessary" military equipment

The soldiers were cautioned about the frequency of sting rays and sharks. The biggest fear, in Chill's mind, was the prospect of being target practice for a sniper. He felt especially vulnerable because the waves were so long. He remembers on several occasions getting ". . . weird thoughts . . . what if there is a V-C with a rifle sitting over there?"

Chill describes those waves as "rolling on forever and ever. I'd never seen anything like it before or since." They were as much as eight to ten feet high and "were so long that you could fall off, grab your board, get up again, and still have a decent ride." What also stands out was the incredible pristine quality of the water. Chill remembers going out on Army patrol boats and "seeing down one hundred feet, as clear as day."

Losing the natural beauty of our own Ocean County is something that weighs heavily on Chill's mind these days. "The bay is polluted, I don't know if it's dying or not. There's so much development around here now. I remember when three-quarters of the people in Ocean County made their living in the bay and it was a good living."

Surfing has been just one part of Chill Paul's interesting life, which has included working in every aspect of the clamming industry, competing in dog-sled racing, guiding duck-hunting parties, and traveling around the world with the armed services. He is proud that he was a founder of the L.B.I.S.A. and is grateful that he has been able to pass on the surfing tradition to his son, Chuck. Of the people that he met through surfing, Stretch Pohl will always stand out in his mind: "Being around Stretch was special. He was a version of Hemingway - a unique guy."

Chill, we think you're pretty special too.

References:

"Tape Talk." *Competition Surf* (Spring 1966): 26.

"Judges Stand III." *Competition Surf* (Spring 1966): 48.

Carl "Tinker" West

The search to find Carl West, a.k.a. Tinker, took me several months. A lot of people knew of him, they just didn't know where he was. Throughout this search, without exception and without prompting, every person I spoke to described him as an "eccentric genius." My interest was heightened when we finally met. Tinker looked normal enough, but he did have a sharp, witty sense of humor as he switched back and forth and elaborated on dozens of subjects. I desperately tried to keep up, picking up on subtle comments, but I suspect quite a few went over my head. I wasn't allowed to take any notes . . . this wasn't an interview yet. Tinker generously agreed to a second meeting and the promise of a photo album filled with pictures of the trip from his native California to the East Coast in 1960, and so our story begins . . .

While enjoying a night of some alcoholic beverages, Gordon Kennerly, Al Warner, John Millington Kemper III, Alan Price, and Tinker West decided it was time for their next adventure. A trip to Mexico was suggested but then voted down since it had already been done. Someone flippantly suggested that they travel to New Jersey to find Earl Eckels. Earl had lived and surfed with the group in El Porto, California, before returning to the East Coast. The group unanimously decided that seeing the look on Earl's face would make the trip worthwhile.

The trip would be no small undertaking. They were short on funds and the only address they had for Earl was Long Beach Island, New Jersey. They collected $50 to purchase a 1950 two-door sedan, and then removed all the seats to fit a mattress and a wooden chair for a driver's seat. It was the only way that they could fit all the surfboards, five people, and Spade, the wonder dog. They siphoned gas all the way from California to New Jersey, storing it at times in additional gasoline holders on the outside of the car. There were some delays along the way since the vehicle caught the attention of many local law enforcement officials across the country.

The group made it in one piece, about six days later, in late August. It was night when they finally drove over the Causeway and decided to pull off the side of the road until morning. Parked in an area of thick cattails and reeds for the night, they didn't count on the attack of the killer mosquitoes, because, quite frankly, they didn't know mosquitoes existed. All they could do was cover their entire bodies from head to toe with blankets while enduring the unforgiving humidity, another East Coast phenomenon. Several of them still have welts on their body to this day from that infamous night.

The mission was completed when the following day they actually found Earl, where else, but at a surfing beach. The next order of business was to find employment that would supply the funds for their return trip to the West Coast. Thanks to locals: Sonny and Wickey Baugh, and Wimpy Paulsworth, the Californians were introduced to the clamming business. They even made enough money to be able to move out of their car into a "cold water flat" above John's Beach Wear in Surf City.

The Californians stayed on LBI about a month, adding to their résumé: East coast surfing, clamming, riding out Hurricane Donna, mixing with the locals at the "old" Dutchmann's Bar, and making friendships that have lasted a life time.

When Tinker returned to California, he worked for Wardy Surfboards in Laguna Beach and also Challenger Surfboards in San Diego. He recognized that almost seventy percent of the boards being made were shipped to the East Coast. Already familiar with the demographics and high density of the greater New York/New Jersey area, manufacturing boards on the East Coast seemed a logical business endeavor.

From 1966 to 1971, Tinker manufactured Challenger Eastern Surfboards, first in Neptune and later in Ocean Township. At the height of his business, he was putting out 70-80 boards per week and working out of a 6,000 square foot warehouse. Much of the business was piece-work, which carried with it a certain business risk if the surf was good and no one felt like working—imagine that! Tinker wholesaled boards as far north as Maine and Massachusetts and down through New York, New Jersey and Virginia. He also had a retail surf shop in Avalon, New Jersey.

(**A**) Cross-country luxury mobile, complete with lots of extras: external fuel tanks, removable lawn chair seating and non-puncture resistant tires (**B**) Learning the East Coast surfer's trade of choice: Clamming (**C**) California crew, including Spade the Wonder Dog, pose outside John's Beach Wear. Their temporary accomodations were in an apartment above. Tinker carved the wooden tiki. This skill was another source of income to help make it back to the West Coast.

Unfortunately, it's difficult to capture the essence of Tinker in one chapter about surfing. His expertise and interests extend to a wide variety of areas. His musical interests led him to urge Vinnie Lopez of "Upstage," an Asbury coffeehouse, to put together a band with some *original* music, something he felt the East Coast bands were lacking. He offered his warehouse for band rehearsals and also found himself designing and building sound systems. Tinker was more than qualified to help with the band's audio engineering needs. (Tinker has a background in physics from El Camino College and UCLA. He is also a member of the New York Academy of Science). The original sound that was discovered belonged to Bruce Springsteen. Tinker also managed Springsteen, when he played in the Steel Mill Band.

Tinker's background in engineering originally led him into the aerospace industry. He worked at Wyle Labs, the primary contractor for "environmental testing" of missile systems. He performed stress and strain analysis for many prototypes that were considered classified at that time. Today, Tinker owns C. West Engineering and Design which advertises: "Specializing in the unique and unusual." His design and fabrication company combines expertise in woodworking, metallurgy, and electronics. Some of his customers have included Carnegie Hall and the Boston Symphony. When not doing that, this Renaissance man is also restoring or sailing old wooden boats. At sixty-five years young (he is fit and doesn't look his age), Tinker still surfs and is up for anything that sounds like it might be an adventure.

> *Tinker was one of the best mechanical shapers I have ever had the pleasure to have known. I had been shaping for five years and met him in New Jersey. He offered me a job and taught me the finer points of using a planer and how to really lay out a surfboard. He was taught by Velzy and Velzy himself says Tinker was one of his best students, an eye for the cleanest, straightest lines, never bumps or twists. Tinker was an electrical engineer by trade and grew up on the space industry of Los Angeles before turning to shaping and building boards. He put this electrical knowledge to work, building sound systems for Bruce, Ike and Tina Turner and James Cotton. He has a design and fabrication studio where he still rigs for the Boston Philharmonic and others—a remarkable genius of a man.*

He has been the most pivotal person in my career as a surfboard craftsman. Without his tutelage, I never would have progressed as far as I have today.

—Jim Phillips, shaper
Phillips Surfboards

The First Surf Shops

SURF SHOP PHENOMENON

Surf shops began to enter the retail market on Long Beach Island during the early 1960s. It all began with Ron DiMenna who initially sold California-manufactured pop-out surfboards on the mainland. Would-be surfers found a few boards outside his father's grocery store. The bigger selection, however, was in Ron's attic in his home in Manahawkin. Still unable to keep up with demand, in the summer of 1961 Ron filled a rented trailer with surfboards and set-up shop on the Causeway entrance to LBI. With that, Ron Jon Surf Shop was born, and the rest is history.

A similar phenomenon was happening at the other end of the island in Beach Haven. The Koseff Family, already proprietors of a department store, began carrying a handful of surfboards in 1963. They also saw potential in the surfing industry and purchased a separate building in order to operate Koseff's Surf Shop from 1965 to 1969. With the resurgence of the longboard phenomenon, Koseff's Surf Shop returned to the island from 1990 to 2000.

Other shops started appearing on LBI like Walters Equipment for the Beach (Ship Bottom) and Acuff Surfboads (North Beach Haven) that were on the scene in 1965. They were followed by shops like Brant Beach Surf Shop (Brant Beach) from 1966 to 1980, which later became Brighton Beach Surf Shop from 1982 to the present; Atlantis Surf Shop (North Beach Haven) from 1968 to 1969; and Rick Surf Shop (Ship Bottom) from 1967 to 1973, formerly Custom Surf Shop (1966). Chito's Surf Shop was a welcome sight for surfers at the northern end of the island from 1969 to 1976.

Each shop had its own distinct following, and most shops had some version of a sponsored surf team. Being a surf team member carried a lot of clout on the island. Surf team members were recognized by the younger generation of aspiring surfers. They were invited to the best beach parties with the "in crowd." In addition to trunks and jackets with the surf team logo, they were eligible for special prices in the respective surf shop.

Anybody who was anybody was seen at a surf shop. The surf shops were a place for young people to make summer cash by either working in retail, fixing surfboards, or giving surf lessons. The surf shops also made arrangements for a host of internationally-recognized shapers and riders to visit LBI. Promoting their products, legends like Dewey Weber, Hobie Alter, Greg Noll, Claude Codgen, Skip Frye, Midget Farrelly, and Johnny Fain all made their way to LBI. They could be found in surf shops, judging surf meets, or their favorite place of all—out in the water . . . surfing LBI.

On the following pages, you'll find the stories of how some of the early surf shops came into existence, and the characters that made it all possible. You will also see ads for surfing products that found their way into department stories in cities like Philadelphia and New York in the mid-60s. It seemed like everyone wanted to jump on the band wagon. The "East Coast Directory" that appeared in the winter 1965 issue of *Surfing East* will give you an idea of how quickly the surfing scene was growing on the East Coast. You'll notice that New Jersey and Long Beach Island in particular had a strong showing right from the start.

Surfing products make it to department stores: Macy's ad for Malibu and Keoki Surfboards. This ad appeared in *The New York Times* on May 23, 1965.

John Wanamaker ad for Catalina Surfers® clothing collection. This ad appeared in *The Sunday Bulletin (Philadelphia)* on May 9, 1965 and advertised an opportunity to meet the world champion tandem surf team of Linda Merrill and Mike Doyle.

East Coast Directory

SURFING EAST 1965

NEW YORK

Beachcomber Surf Shop
191 A Broadway
Amityville

Crestwood Surfing
215 Nassau Street
Hewlett

Custom Billiards
126 W. Main Street
Babylon

Down Under Surf Shop
1250 Montauk Hwy.
Copiague

Emilios Ski Shop
112-32 Queens Blvd.
Forest Hills

Hannon Surfboards
215 Middle Neck Rd.
Great Neck

Jamaica Skin Divers
169-09 Jamaica Ave.
Jamaica

Kohl's Surf Shop
7 Gilbert Road West
Great Neck

Micris Surfboards
Railroad & Broadway
Greenlawn

Olympic Ski Shops
1107 Northern Blvd.
Manhasset

Pipeline East
82 Mill Road
W. Hampton Beach

Post Ski & Sport Shop
30 W. Merrick Road
Valley Stream

Post Ski & Sport Shop
1131 Lexington Avenue
New York City

Sealawn Prod. Co.
504 Park Place
Long Beach

Surf City U.S.A.
Mid Island Plaza
Hicksville

Franklin Avenue
Hempstead

Sport Trails
1537 Northern Blvd.
Manhasset

Snow Haus Ski Shop
246 N. Franklin Street
Hempstead

Snow Haus Ski Shop
Route #110
Huntington

NEW JERSEY

[Acuff Surfboards
1501 N. Beach Haven
Long Beach Island]

[Bill's Custom Boards
Shiphottom
New Jersey]

Custom Surf Shop
507 Grand Central Ave.
Lavalette

Dickie Doo Surfboards
470 Second Avenue
Long Branch

Fletcher Surf Shop
Rt. #70 & Green Tree Road
Cherry Hill

Keller's Surf Shop
1605 Grand Central Ave.
Lavallette

Koneff's, Inc.
Third & Bay Avenues
Beach Haven

Manatee Sea Center
12th & Ocean Avenues
Belmar

Manatee Sea Center
14th & Asbury Avenues
Ocean City

The Mogul Surf Shop
Main & Sheridan Avenues
Clifton

Perdue's Sport Shop
158 Franklin Avenue
Ridgewood

[Ron-Jon Surf Shop
12 Lyle Avenue
Manahawkin]

[Ron-Jon Surf Shop
Causeway
Ship Bottom]

Schuck Surfboards
2653 Nottingham Way Rear
Trenton

Scoop's Sporting Goods
Rio Grande & New Jersey
Wildwood

Steger's Sun & Surf Shop
Beach Drive
Cape May

[Stretch Pohl Surfboards
Surf City]

Surf and Sand Surf Shop
8th & Atlantic Avenues
Ocean City

Surf and Sand Surf Shop
106 96th Street
Stone Harbor

Surfer Shop
610 Ocean Avenue
Pt. Pleasant

Surf Shack
Route #37
Pelican Island

Surfers Supply
3101 Asbury Avenue
Ocean City

Village Store
Main Street
Whitehouse Station

[Walter's Surf Rentals
418 Long Beach Blvd.
Ship Bottom]

DELAWARE

Eastern Surfer
246 Delaware Avenue
Harrington

MARYLAND

Eastern Surfer
18th Street & Boardwalk
Ocean City

Paul's Aqua Shop
204 St. Louis Avenue
Ocean City

Maryland Surfboards
5436 Harford Road
Baltimore

Triangle Sporting Goods
Baltimore

The Sportsmen
Bethesda

VIRGINIA

Butch's Surf Shop
207 19th Street
Virginia Beach

City Sports Shop
Alexandria

Long's Sport Shop
Hampton

Morgan Patch Shop
200 22nd Street
Virginia Beach

Rosi Surfboards
208 23rd Street
Virginia Beach

Smith & Holland Surf Shop
204 22nd Street
Virginia Beach

Virginia Beach Hardware
Virginia Beach Blvd.
Virginia Beach

Western Auto Supply
600 Virginia Beach Blvd.
Virginia Beach

NORTH CAROLINA

Atlantic Surf Shop
Kure Beach

SOUTH CAROLINA

East Coast Surfboards
Box 268
Carolina Beach

Divines Sporting Goods
Myrtle Beach

GEORGIA

Davis Marine
Macon

Johnson's Surf Shop
Box 8
Pawley's Island

FLORIDA

Boca Raton Surf Shop
707 E. Palmetto Road
Boca Raton

Buck's Surf Shop
2080 N.E. 2nd Street
Deerfield Beach

Caribbean Surfboards
210 E. Atlantic Avenue
Delray Beach

Campbell Surfboards
7419 New Haven Avenue
Melbourne

Challenger Marine
1331 Biscayne Blvd.
North Miami Beach

Chuck's Hut
2209 N.E. 163rd Street
North Miami Beach

Daytona Beach Surf Shop
506 Main Street
Daytona Beach

Delray Surfboards
217 East Atlantic
Delray Beach

Diver's Haven
1530 Cordova Road
Ft. Lauderdale

Dive 'n' Spear
906 N. Ocean Drive
Hollywood Beach

Dude's Surf Shop
1200 S. Federal Hwy.
Fort Lauderdale

Flying Dutchman Surf Shop
324-A Ocean Avenue
Melbourne Beach

Glass Research, Inc.
924 North Lane Avenue
Jacksonville

MAINE

Bikini Surf Shop
3 Acorn Street
York Beach

MASSACHUSETTS

Machine & Marine Service
Vineyard Haven
Martha's Vineyard

Nauset Surf
Nauset Beach Road
(At Packet Landing Inn)
Box 1011
Orleans, Cape Cod

Paul's East Coast Surf Shop
Village Green, Rt. #6
North Eastham, Cape Cod

Seacraft Sporting Goods
Church Street
Wilmington

Snow's Cycle Shop
37 Main St.
Nantucket

RHODE ISLAND

Block Island Surf Shop
Block Island

Narraganset Surf Shop
3 Kingston Road
Narraganset

Ryan's Sporting Goods
Newport

CONNECTICUT

Dick's Ski & Scuba Shop
Rt. #6 & Plainsville Ave.
Farmington

W. C. Spicer
916 Shennecosset
Groton

"East Coast Directory" as it appeared in *Surfing East* magazine, 1965 Winter Edition. Long Beach Island businesses are indicated by the box.

RON JON SURF SHOP

What do you get when you put together a Baptist minister, a high school student, and the son of a grocery store owner? You get a surfing retail store dynasty known the world over as Ron Jon Surf Shop. Ron DiMenna, who has remained an integral part of this surfing business since the beginning, would say about Earl Comfort, "This is the guy who started it all." And that's where our story begins . . .

The Reverend Earl Comfort moved into town with his wife JoAnn in 1958. He would pastor the Manahawkin Baptist Church until 1970. Even though Earl was Philadelphia born and raised, he was no stranger to the Jersey Shore. Earl's father was a musician who performed with a jazz band at summer entertainment spots in Ocean City and Cape May. This gave the whole family an opportunity to vacation at the beach from June through September each year. For three of these summer seasons, Earl worked as a lifeguard with the Ocean City Beach Patrol. There he fine-tuned his water skills which included "surfing" with the lifeboats, bodysurfing, and, if you can picture this, "belly skidding"—running as fast as you could on the water's edge and then throwing yourself, belly first, onto the cushion of water at the water's edge. This was apparently an early version of modern skimboarding, minus the equipment. A love for the ocean was instilled forever, and probably a few bruises as well.

Earl estimates that it was about 1960 that "a group of guys from California had come through and were making surfboards at the Old Fishery that was just off the Causeway." This group surfed a few times in Ship Bottom that Earl got to see. Not too long after that, he found William "Wimpy" Paulsworth building boards at the Clam Stand on old Bay Avenue.

The wheels started turning for Earl as he thought to himself, "I can do that." He bought two blocks of styrofoam and redwood for a stringer from the Tuckerton Lumber Company. Everything was coming together nicely until he heard some "strange crackling noises" and realized that the resin he was using was melting the styrofoam. Thinking quickly, he switched to epoxy resin and salvaged the board. Earl admits that the board had at least one small flaw: it leaked.

Proudly garnishing the roof of his car, it didn't take long for this surfboard to draw some interest. His next door neighbor, Ron DiMenna, was one of the first people to inquire about it. When Earl explained that it was a surfboard, Ron said, "You mean like in California or Hawaii?" That very day, Ron was heading out to the beach with him to try this new sport. "Back then we didn't know about coming in on the wave sideways," Earls remembers. "We would just get up and go straight in. After four or five waves, we would have to drain the board."

Ron grew up in South Orange, but spent his early life in Manahawkin. His father Felix owned a grocery store/butcher shop in town. Ron was working for his father at the time he met Earl Comfort. Ron had recently returned from his tour of duty with the U.S. Marine Corps where he served as a member of the elite White House Honor Guard.

Two houses away from all the commotion at Earl's house, lived John Spodofora. His interest was sparked as well. He already had some background "standing up on water" through his expertise waterskiing. John, who was still in high school, had the boat and equipment to teach them waterskiing if they taught him to surf.

It soon became obvious that one surfboard for the three of them just wasn't enough. Ron and John took some measurements from Earl's board and began trying their hand at homemade boards. They got some help from John's father who was a cabinet maker. He helped them work with jigs to lay up the redwood stringers. The real challenge was finding a place with a constant 70° air temperature to cure the resin. Ron's wife and John's mother had to be convinced that their kitchens and living rooms were the ideal place for building surfboards.

Earl was actually the first one in the group to 'break down' and buy a new board. He saw an ad in a surfing magazine and ordered one from California. Rumors began circulating around

Southern Regional High School that "Reverend Earl Comfort had one of those new surfboards." It wasn't long before kids were knocking at his front door and asking just to see the board. Ron couldn't help but notice the constant parade of young people to the Comforts' home. Ron remarked, "Earl this is going to go."

According to John, "After Ron and I made our own surfboards we had numerous individuals asking us to make additional boards. In our early enthusiasm we decided to come up with the brand name of 'Ron Jon.' We drew up the first decal representing Ron and myself for our early surfboards. However, we quickly saw there was no way we could meet the high demand for boards by making them ourselves. That is when Ron decided to order some pop-outs from California."

When Ron spoke to his father about buying new surfboards from California, Felix DiMenna gave him the following advice: "Buy three, sell two at a profit, yours will be free." Some of the pop-out boards from California were displayed in front of the family's grocery store. A large number of boards were sold from the attic of Ron DiMenna's home. It became obvious that Ron needed a bigger area to display surfboards to accommodate the growing throng of new surfers. The year was 1961 when Ron decided to move the surfboards sale about five miles east, to the entrance of Long Beach Island. Located on the Causeway and Central Avenue, Ron filled a rented red, white, and blue trailer with surfboards. With this, Ron Jon Surf Shop was officially opened, and the rest is history.

John Spodofora spent weekends and the summer of his senior year of high school helping Ron DiMenna run the rental and sales business out of this trailer. Former customers were also supplied with boards to open their own shops at other spots on the East Coast.

Ron Jon Surf Shop sponsored a Dewey Weber Surf Team. Like other teams on the island, they competed in the Northern East Coast Division from Rhode Island to Virginia. They didn't have a consistent group of competitors. Their ace in the hole was always Hawaiian Ralph Hawn, stationed out of Maguire Air Force Base. Ralph dazzled the locals with moves they had never seen before. Unfortunately, Ralph was surfing at the expense of the Air Force. They didn't take kindly to an AWOL soldier helping the East Coast surfing cause. Ralph disappeared from the island and no one seems to know what ever happened to him.

What wasn't disappearing was the passion for surfing on Long Beach Island, or the East Coast in general. According to an article that Ron DiMenna wrote for *International Surfing*: "In one season, Ron Jon Surf Shop sold more than a thousand boards, while scores of others were rented." Ron DiMenna decided to open a second store—the "One of a Kind" Ron Jon Surf Shop in Cocoa Beach, Florida in 1963. At the same time, John Spodofora's connection with the business aspect of surfing was overshadowed by his pursuit of an engineering degree at Drexel University. John temporarily moved from the area to pursue his professional goals.

Robert Baugher, who began working at Ron Jon Surf Shop in 1965, was gradually given more and more business responsibility by Ron DiMenna. Baugher eventually became Ron Jon's president while DiMenna preferred a reclusive lifestyle, including considerable time spent abroad in Australia. Baugher is credited with making the company a household name. The Ron Jon name is recognized worldwide for its huge selection of board sports equipment as well as active lifestyle apparel. Baugher remained with the company until 1998. Under his reign, the LBI location grew to 8,100 square feet. Besides garnishing the title of "The Original," the LBI store also displays a 24' surfboard which is the largest surfboard in the world.

The Cocoa Beach location also expanded to become a high-tech shopping mall, encompassing 52,000 square feet of retail space. It is the town's top tourist destination, attracting more than one million visitors annually. This latter location is advertised as being "open 24 hours a day, 365 days a year, just like the beach."

Retired Walt Disney Company executive Ed Moriarty became the next president from 1998 to the present. He opened new retail sites in Orange, California (1998) and Ft. Lauderdale, Florida (1999).

Ron Jon Surf Shop has been involved with numerous charitable ventures over the years. The list includes an annual surfing contest held in Brevard County, Florida, for the National Kidney Foundation. The business has also sponsored many anti-drug campaigns, especially in schools in the New Jersey area. Ron Jon advertisements on billboards and radio commercials have proudly displayed D.A.R.E. (Drug Abuse Resistance Education) messages. Ron DiMenna was inducted into the East Coast Legends Hall of Fame on January 10, 1998.

References:

DiMenna, Ronald. "Long Beach Island on the Atlantic." *International Surfing* (June1969): 52-55.

http://www.ronjons.com/thecompany/companyhistory.htm

http://www.ronjons.com/thecompany/corpprofile.htm

RON JON SURF SHOP
The trailer where it all began in 1961 (A)
Circa 1966 (B)
Circa 2000 (C)

CAUSEWAY, SHIP BOTTOM
LONG BEACH ISLAND, N. J.

(609) 494-1141

RESIDENCE (609) 597-7151

SPECIALISTS IN FIBERGLASS SURFBOARDS
RETAIL & WHOLESALE

PRICES EFFECTIVE SEPTEMBER 15, 1965 - SUBJECT TO CHANGE WITHOUT NOTICE.

CUSTOM SURFBOARDS

QUALITY   CRAFTSMANSHIP

PRICES INCLUDE THESE OR ANY OTHER CUSTOM BOARDS LISTED IN MY ADVERTISEMENTS.

HANSEN, DEWEY WEBER, HAWAII, YATER, GORDIE, HARDY, JACOBS, MILLER		RON JON	
$140	UNDER 8'6"	$120	
145	8'7" - 9'	125	
150	9'1" - 9'5"	130	
155	9'6" - 10'	135	
160	10' - 10'5"	140	

ABOVE PRICES INCLUDE

ANY CUSTOM SHAPE DESIRED		½" BALSA ½" REDWOOD	(HANSEN ONLY)
CLEAR FINISH		T BAND	(DEWEY WEBER)
2 LAYERS 10 OZ. CLOTH		REGULAR GLASS FIN OR SPEED FIN	
4 LAYERS ON RAILS		WOOD FIN	(HANSEN & GORDIE ONLY)
HAND RUBBED RAILS TO HIGH GLOSS FINISH		GLASS TAIL BLOCK	(RON JON & HANSEN)
CHOICE: 3/4" REDWOOD OR 1" BALSA STRINGER		WOOD TAIL BLOCK	(DEWEY SEDER)

HIGH DENSITY POLYURETHANE FOAM

EXTRAS

COLORS			STRINGERS		
PINSTRIPES	EACH	$2.00	REQUIRING EXTRA CUT		$6.00
SOLID COLOR		10.00	NOT REQUIRING EXTRA CUT		4.00
COLOR OR DESIGN	ONE SIDE	6.00	BALSA	PER INCH	3.00
	BOTH SIDES	10.00			
EXTRA COLORS	EACH	3.00	FANCY WOOD FINS		5.00
SINGLE BAND AROUND BOARD UP TO 6"		6.00	FANCY TAIL BLOCK		5.00
COLOR ON COLOR		2.00	NOSE BLOCK		5.00

SHIPPING: FREE DELIVERY ANY PLACE IN NEW JERSEY AND PENNSYLVANIA. FOR SPECIAL ORDERS ALLOW 3 WEEKS. LARGE SELECTION FROM STOCK AVAILABLE AT SHOWROOM IMMEDIATELY. DEPOSIT REQUIRED ON ALL ORDERS. BALANCE OF PAYMENT DUE UPON DELIVERY. PLEASE ENCLOSE $10.00 DEPOSIT WITH MAIL ORDERS.

21'= off hest

VENTURA SURFBOARDS (ONE YEAR GUARANTEE)

SIZE	SURFER WEIGHT	SHARK	TIKI & MAUI HAND SHAPED	STING RAY & OLE HAND SHAPED	VENTURA & HAWAII HAND SHAPED	BLANKS
9'0"	110 - 135	$89	$105	$116	$125	$27
9'4"	135 - 160	89	110	121	130	28
9'8"	160 - 185	89	113	127	133	29
10'0"	185 & OVER	89	117	129	138	30

COLORS	RED	AQUA	ORANGE	BLUE

NEW LOW SHIPPING AND HANDLING CHARGES - ADD ONLY $10.00

CARTOP CARRIERS		$10.95 & $13.95	POCKET SIZE SURFBOARD WAX	40¢ BAR
ALL DECALS	MED. .35	.60 LRG.	RON JON TEE SHIRTS	$2.00
COMPLETE SURFBOARD REPAIR KITS	4.95		RON JON SWEAT SHIRTS	3.75
WET SURF VESTS AVAILABLE*				

Reverend Earl Comfort

They say it's not easy being a minister's wife. You would have to ask JoAnn Comfort which has been harder, being a minister's wife or a surfer's wife. Earl remembers positioning two surfboards in their living room the better part of one winter. It was the only place that he had enough room to work on his homemade surfboards with a constant 70° air temperature for curing the resin. Earl can still vividly picture JoAnn, bent sideways at her waist, trying to see past the boards to the television set. Then there was the time that JoAnn will never let him forget. She was in the hospital and in labor with their fourth child. Earl used the opportunity to try to convince JoAnn that they could afford the $40 needed to purchase a used surfboard from Wimpy down at the Clam Shack. According to Earl, "It was so much better than what we could make."

Earl eventually got that used board, a Jacobs double-stringer. But, like most surfers, he couldn't stop there. He later saw surfboards advertised in a magazine and ordered a new one from California. When the young people in the neighborhood heard about the board, they started coming by Earl's house. Ron DiMenna couldn't help noticing all the interest and saw the business potential involved. Earl remembers Ron speaking to him about going into business together. Earl politely declined and continued to go about his business of saving souls.

Earl found surfing to be a "wonderful springboard" to get the ear of young people and introduce them to the message of Jesus Christ. "Surfing was the crack in the door that helped overcome resistance. It gave me a tremendous opportunity to speak to young people about the Good News."

What did his congregation think about a surfing reverend? Well, there was the time that Earl's pearling surfboard left a sizeable laceration on his forehead. Speaking from the pulpit that next Sunday and wearing a white patch on his forehead, he simply said, "I don't want anyone to say a word about this."

If Earl could have great success speaking to young people about Christ, how would he fare speaking to the five mayors of LBI about allowing surfing on its summer beaches? As one of the founding members of the Long Beach Island Surfing Association, Earl attended town council meetings along with other "respectable" community members. At first, the mayors were intent on keeping the "long blonde-haired delinquents" out of their communities. The unrelenting voice of Dr. Rev. Comfort began to silence some of the criticism about the debauchery thought to be associated with the sport. The mayors were finally willing to allow surfing on the beaches "before and after the beaches were open."

The surfing association grew in number to over two hundred members at its peak. Club members had quilted jackets with the *Long Beach Island Surfing Assc.* patch on the sleeve. There were monthly meetings which usually included an 8mm surfing film. "That's when the kids went crazy. These movies from the West Coast showed the kids that there was more to wave-riding than just coming straight in."

Earl's passion for surfing has continued throughout his entire life. His children and grandchildren share his enthusiasm for the water. His son Geoffrey, of Florida, continues to enjoy surfing despite a motorcycle accident on LBI that resulted in a lower extremity amputation. Geoffrey was recently invited to the Cocoa Beach Surfing Invitational to raise greater awareness of surfing for the disabled. Sons Chris and Greg are ministers in New Jersey and New Hampshire, respectively. They both find time to surf when they can. Speaking of his son (we won't tell you which one), the Reverend Earl Comfort says, "I've introduced you to two things in my life, Jesus Christ and surfing. Sometimes I'm not sure which one takes precedence."

A freak accident when Earl was sixty-seven resulted in the fusion of four vertebrae in his neck and a titanium plate. His doctors have remained adamant about restricting his return to surfboarding. In Earl's unrelenting style, he did manage to convince them to allow him to return to bodysurfing.

When asked to summarize why he loves surfing, Earl shared these thoughts:

> Variety . . . one wave is as different as the next. I don't think there's any other sport quite like it. I've skied before, but it's not the same thing. Surfing is a challenge because no wave is ever the same. When you surf there is fluid motion and you are part of God's wonderful creation—the ocean. There is a lot of companionship. There is a thrill when the waves get big. Those first two to three seconds when you first get up . . . what a rush!

Ron DiMenna and Reverend Earl Comfort, second and third from the left, pose with other wave enthusiasts. Both men were instrumental in promoting the sport on LBI through endeavors such as the Long Beach Island Surfing Association. Pictured is an original patch given to all members of the organization.

John Spodofora

John was a junior at Southern Regional High School in Manahawkin, New Jersey when he started surfing with Earl Comfort and Ron DiMenna. John found himself "obsessed" with surfing. He was constantly buying surfing magazines, watching surfing movies, and doing book reports on surfing. "It's all I wanted to do."

The surfing obsession led he and other surfers to push the limits in the cold northeast water. The only wetsuits available at the time were diving suits. John remembers, "There was no lining and they were always ripping. Even when you had them on you still felt like you might freeze to death." That early group, desperate to stay warm, even tried several non-conventional methods. "We would place vaseline all over our bodies to try to repel the cold water or 'Ben Gay' stuff to try to feel some artificial warmth." John remembers shaking so bad in the water he could barely talk. Nevertheless, it was a small price to pay, to be out in the water.

John recalls the early days and the kinship of those first LBI surfers. "We all knew each other then. I was one of the youngest in our group. I didn't even have a car, but everyone generously drove me wherever I had to go." John remembers trying to "shoot the Steel Pier" like they'd seen the California surfers do in movies picturing Huntington Beach. They broke a few boards that way and almost a few body parts.

Then, there were the calmer days when you could "really get to know someone" waiting out in the line-up during the long lulls in between sets. John fondly recalls the "philosophical talks" with Reverend Comfort on just such days. Another experience which will always stand-out in John's mind was the foggy morning he spent surfing with Wimpy Paulsworth. Out of the corner of his eye, John noticed porpoises circling them. These magnificent creatures then began nudging their boards. "The whole experience was so surreal, especially with the mist and fog. It felt special just being there. I didn't want a wave to come, I just enjoyed being there and having these wonderful animals touch us."

Unfortunately, John's days at the beach were numbered. He was forced to spend time inland when he pursued his engineering degree at Drexel University in Philadelphia. With the conflict in Vietnam escalating, John enlisted in the U.S. Navy. Up until that time, John had enjoyed many water activities, not only surfing and water-skiing but also scuba diving and working on commercial fishing boats. He was about to learn the Navy's version of what "water activities" meant.

John's first assignment was at the Great Lakes Naval Station in Illinois. Feeling landlocked from his beloved ocean, he wandered along the shoreline of the Great Lakes. He could hardly believe his eyes. There were several surfers out surfing "wind waves." He begged to use one of the surfboards that was there. He had on a pair of blue jeans which he quickly cut off to make into a pair of shorts. That day he surfed all afternoon.

Much of John's work was in the submarine service in naval intelligence. Several of his assignments are considered "classified" to this day. Through the Navy, John had a chance to live and surf in California as well as Puerto Rico. In the latter, he discovered not only Rincon Beach but also noticed a Ron Jon surfboard one day in the water. The Ron Jon phenomenon had already moved far from its humble roots in a trailer in New Jersey.

John has never forgotten his roots. He returned to Manahawkin with his wife, Helen, and raised a daughter, Kari, and son, Derek, who have also enjoyed surfing. He is still employed by the Navy, working as a cost analyst at the Lakehurst Naval Air Station. He is perhaps most recognized, however, for the work he has accomplished while serving as a councilman in Stafford Township since May 1988.

Politics were never actually part of John's plan. It all happened when he recognized that a proposed town house project would compromise Stafford Township's storm water management system. He expressed his concerns to Mayor Carl Block who offered him the opportunity to come up with a better plan. Well, not only did John come up with a better plan, but that plan has been impressing people ever since. John created a unique type of ground water recharge system. It is designed to catch water in the storm drains and then percolate runoff back into the ground via perforated pipes. This system has successfully kept irrigation ponds, lakes, and wells full, even during droughts. John's insight and commitment made him a natural choice to head a new Environmental Commission that Mayor Block created.

Under John's leadership, the Stafford Township Environmental Commission has won more environmental awards at the state and national level than any other commission in the country. In 1994, John accepted the Environmental Protection Agency (EPA) National Award of Excellence. This award was presented in Chicago by the King of Sweden to recognize the storm water management design. In 1995, the National Geographic Society documented Stafford's environmental accomplishments. Stafford's environmental ordinances have even been translated into six different languages per the work of Gale Wyman, who represents an international group of scientists and engineers known as US-AID.

There are two additional accolades that John is especially proud of, though he tries to shy away from praise. One of these is the John Spodofora Award created by the Stafford Township School System. It is given each year to a boy who shows the greatest love for the environment. The other award is the National Theodore Roosevelt Conservation Award that was presented by President George W. Bush in 1990. This award was for the successful restoration of Manahawkin Lake, considered by the EPA to be the most successful project of its kind in the nation. John accepted this award on national television during a special ceremony at the White House. The President called Stafford Township's storm water management plan "one of the thousand points of light."

John's schedule is a hectic one between his family, work, civic duties, and environmental speaking engagements. It doesn't allow much time for surfing these days, but he keeps it in perspective this way: "I've had an opportunity to take a lot from the ocean. I feel that it's only right to give something back. If you enjoy it then you have to value it and protect it." John believes that most surfers are strong advocates for the environment. "Ocean quality is at the very core of surfing. Surfers are often the first ones to see first-hand the causes and effects of pollution."

Each of us had our own reason to be drawn to the sport of surfing and each of us were impacted in different ways by our involvement in this sport of the 'Ancient Hawaiian Kings.' For me, it was a sport of individuality, something that put me on a one-to-one basis with the ocean and the eco-systems it supported. This was not a team sport nor was it a sport that involved competition, scores, or any rigid rules. Equipment needs were simple: a surfboard, some wax, maybe a wetsuit. We surfed for the love of the sport, we moved with the rhythm of the waves, the winds, and the tides. You couldn't compete against the sea. Instead, when you caught a wave, you became part of the wave. The perfect wave was a gift. It's power, direction, and size, along with your skill level, would determine the quality of the ride.

Surfing taught us to read the waves . . . to understand what conditions made the waves better in one location over another. We learned one can not tame the ocean and that it demanded our respect. We also learned how to recognize subtle changes in the water quality, its causes and impact on sea life.

For me, surfing along with scuba diving gave me a love and respect for the ocean that I still feel compelled to share. However, it is also a private thing buried deep inside of me that I feel would be impossible to explain. I only hope that the new generation of surfers takes the time to enjoy the sport for what it is . . . that they take the time to allow themselves to become one with the sea and its powerful waves.

- John Spodofora

KOSEFF'S SURF SHOP

If you lived on the southern end of Long Beach Island in the early 1960s, chances are you bought something from Koseff's Department Store. Located on 3rd Street and Bay Avenue in Beach Haven, the store sold hardware, fishing and tackle gear, and a little bit of everything else, or almost everything. Renny and Ernie, the next generation of Koseffs, would see to it that a growing interest in the surfing lifestyle would also become part of the family business.

Renny readily admits that when they entered the surfing business in 1963, they didn't know one board manufacturer from another. These were the days before surfing trade shows and surfboard reps with fax machines and websites. The only major resource in the 1960s was a surfing magazine filled with California-based products. The Koseffs leafed through the magazine and ultimately found their product . . . Greg Noll Surfboards. The name didn't mean a whole lot at the time, but, by chance or destiny, it would turn out to be the perfect match. It not only brought a well-known West Coast board to LBI but it also brought the legend himself on several occasions.Greg Noll spoke about those early days during an interview for the surfing video, *Drenched in Devotion* (2001):

> *Coming back here (East Coast), as a board manufacturer, one of my first impressions was the whole Koseff Family, Ernie and Renny. I remember going to a family dinner they invited me to that was traditional with their heritage. It was absolutely classic. Then we invited Ron Hartmann and Renny to our place (California). They hung around about a month. Really, more than anything it was not only close friends but from the first time I met those guys I realized they were special. The relationship was, and still is today, more of family than anything else.*

Renny was 20 years old when he decided to take some time off from college to travel to California with Ron Hartmann from Beach Haven. They spent about five months on the West Coast, learning the "nuts and bolts" of the surfing industry. When Renny returned, a decision was made to purchase a florist shop located immediately behind their department store. This new site became the home of Koseff's Surf Shop which operated from 1965 to 1969. The building was torn down in 1970.

Koseff's Surf Shop did not open again until 1990. In that year, Renny's son, Zach, convinced the family to operate one of the retail spaces in Pier 18 Mall as a surf shop. Owned and operated by the Koseff family, the mall was located on the site of the earlier businesses.

Koseff's Surf Shop rode the wave of the longboard comeback through the 1990s, featuring surfing apparel and boards by Lance Carson, Harbour, Bing, Eaton, and you guessed it, Greg Noll. Sadly, the surf shop closed in 2000 when the mall was sold to become Silver Sun Mall.

Koseff's Surf Shop was always more than just a *place* on LBI. For many, it was a *time* in their youth. It's legacy will especially live through the stories of the members of its surf team who fondly remember not only all the craziness and fun, but also the kindness of the Koseff family.

The Koseff-Greg Noll Surf Team competed in the "Northern East Coast" division which encompassed the area from Rhode Island to Virginia. The team surfed competitively from early spring to mid-summer, spending most weekends on the road. A Ford Econoline van was graciously donated for use on contest trips. Koseff Surf Team was painted on the side, along with advertisements for products like Dutch Boy Paints.

The group enjoyed a lot of team success. This was due in part to their comparatively large group of talented female surfers. Some teams didn't have any female competitors. Meanwhile, it wasn't uncommon for the Koseff Team to sweep all three places in the women's category. Don't be misled, though, the Koseff Team had not only quantity, but quality as well. Competitors like Diane Pinnix, Bonnie Roth, and Barb Oughton had what it took to even go on and brave Hawaiian surf. (Check out the chapter: "Ladies of LBI")

The men's division was led by Californian, **DEAN EDWARD.** Greg Noll was instrumental in getting Dean to the East Coast.

Dean initially came to LBI to spend the summer and assist with ding repairs at Koseff's Surf Shop. When Dean came east, he not only fixed surfboards, but also made quite a few for Koseff's rental fleet. They were nothing fancy—solid colors (red, yellow, green), without a logo. Dean identified his work by writing the size, date, and his name on the stringer. You could also tell his work by the two layers of 10 ounce cloth he used to minimize the damage to these heavily-used rental boards.

Working at the surf shop, Dean always drew a crowd. It was a thrill for the young people to see boards being shaped and glassed before their eyes. Locals, like Huckleberry, remember spending every spare moment as a kid, either surfing or watching Dean work on surfboards.

Dean was equally well-known for his surfing talent. He was always one of the top finishers for the Koseff-Greg Noll Surf Team. As fellow teammate Sam Baugh remembers, "He was an idol to us all as kids. He was the one who taught us to do a bottom turn." Dean was very gracious about sharing his West Coast surfing skills with the rest of the team until he returned to California.

Twin brothers, **SAM & ERNIE BAUGH** were early standouts on the Koseff Surf Team. They started surfing at 12 years old, competing in the Junior Men's Division. Sam recalls that many of the team members rode Mickey Dora Cats. "It wasn't hard back then to ride the nose on those boards. When you're an eighty pound kid, not only can you walk the nose but you can jump up and down on it too."

The Baughs remember the thrill as kids when Greg Noll traveled with the team from New Jersey to a competition in Virginia Beach. Another favorite story was the time that Sam was the only person from the Koseff Team to qualify for the finals at a Virginia Beach contest. At the same time, a hurricane was making its way toward the coast of Cape Hatteras. Dejected by their losses, but enticed by the thrill of riding hurricane swells, the team traveled on to North Carolina. Sam was left to fend for himself and spent a night sleeping under the pier in Virginia Beach. He took it all in stride. After all, they did stop and pick him up on the way home.

Both brothers did well in surfing competition. Sam won both the Junior Men's LBI Championship and Garden State Championship in 1964. Another big thrill was beating Gary Propper at a surf meet contested in Long Island, New York. This was no easy feat. Propper surfed for the Surfboards Hawaii Team out of Satellite Beach, Florida. This team was consistently the number one team on the East Coast in the 1960s. Propper himself won five consecutive East Coast championships. He was subsequently inducted into the East Coast Legends Hall of Fame in its inaugural year -1996. (An interesting aside is that after competitive surfing, Propper went into show business and made it big with the cartoon, *Teenage Mutant Ninja Turtles*).

But back to the Baughs . . . Sam and Ernie, at seventeen years old, traveled with their cousin George Baugh to California and then on to Hawaii. In Hawaii, they chipped in and bought a station wagon for $80. They lived in that vehicle, even avoiding some minor details like getting tags and registration. They drove around the island of Maui for six months, making ends meet through carpentry jobs.

Sam recalls getting out of the ocean after a session with waves the best that any of them had ever seen. Just then, walking down the cliffs were Jock Sutherland and "Buddy Boy" who had walked down specifically "to see for themselves who these maniacs were" who had been surfing for about four hours. "Don't you know," they asked, "that the tide is just getting right? It should start to get good now."

The brothers continued to travel throughout their lives, visiting places like Portugal, Spain, Morocco, and the Canary Islands. Some of Sam's fondest memories were of Puerto Rico where he spent some thirty winters surfing. Sam was practically a local there. His picture appeared in *International Surfing* magazine in 1969, while surfing an area known as Crashboat.

Crashboat is one of only a few sand bottom breaks in Puerto Rico and is infamous for its hollow wave formed by a sand build-up from a t-shaped pier. About a hundred yards long, this pier was once used for re-fueling PT boats and oil tankers. Surfers have given it new usefulness as a place to tie off a rope with an inner tube attached to it. Sam recalls that it worked well to maintain position despite the unmerciful current that ran through the area.

It was all one could do to stay in position for these picture-perfect 10' to 12' foot tube rides.

Other memories of Puerto Rico include the 25' close-outs of Rincon that carried with them 10' of foam to paddle through. Perhaps even more treacherous was the break at Gas Chambers where 20' waves would suddenly jump another 10' as the result of a powerful surge of backwash. The result was unwary surfers being precariously hurled toward the cliffs. Sam recalls being out one day and seeing one person dislocate their shoulder and then another break their leg. The next one, "Well, they took him away in an ambulance. We were never sure what happened to him."

And whatever happened to the Baughs? They're still on LBI and working in carpentry. They've long since given their Greg Noll Surf Team clothing away to a girl they wanted to impress . . . but now wish they hadn't. Roger Bakst was the LBI'er who memorialized their big wave riding in Puerto Rico, and that's where we go next . . .

ROGER BAKST was born in Newark and spent his youth between New Jersey and Alaska. The first time he ever surfed was in 1959 in Hawaii when he was sixteen. He was vacationing with his family at the Royal Hawaiian Hotel in Waikiki and used a 10' rental surfboard. It was the first and only time someone had to explain to him to put wax on the top of the board.

In the Spring of 1962, Roger visited Bob Schlorer on LBI. Bob was Roger's classmate from Franklin and Marshall College in Lancaster, Pennsylvania. Bob's father was a councilman in Surf City. Roger noticed a surfboard and asked Bob how he could get one. Bob suggested a man named Stretch Pohl who was making custom boards in Ship Bottom. Stretch graciously spoke to Roger. "He guided me in the nuances of surfboard design and construction and even suggested I visit Ron DiMenna in Manahawkin who had some straight from California pop-outs which I could use for comparison." Roger's first board ended up being a 10' Stretch Pohl surfboard, with his customary 40 ounces of cloth on the rails. "After that I was hooked and found every reason I could to get to the island."

For ten plus years, not only Roger's play, but also his work, revolved around surfing. Roger worked one summer for Ron Jon's, several summers for Koseff's, and one summer for Roger Holden's shop in Harvey Cedars. Roger was also co-captain of the Koseff Surf Team for one year. During this time, Roger met the publishers of *Competition Surf* magazine, Ed Greevey and Jim Joiner. Roger soon found himself working for the magazine as a photographer and ad manager. He was also a contributing writer, commonly covering the East Coast competition scene.

Roger was also a contributing writer and photographer for *Surfing* and *Surfing East*. He was a public relations man for Doug Fiske in 1969 when Doug produced a surf film, "The World of Eastern Surfing." Roger promoted the film and arranged showings from Maine to Florida.

Once in Florida, Roger managed Oceanside Surf Shop in Cocoa Beach for six years. This shop is no longer in existence. His background in telecommunications eventually led him to work at WTAI-AM and WTAI-FM stations in Melbourne, Florida. He worked there for two years where he was a disc jockey and promotions manager. Today, he is a real estate broker in the Cocoa Beach area and still surfs his G&S, 7'4" single fin. If you ever have any real estate questions in that area, look him up at ERA Showcase Properties, and tell him *Surfing LBI* sent you.

> *Many business-related surf trips to Florida culminated in my moving to Cocoa Beach, in 1969, but my fondest surf memories are of LBI—especially early morning go-outs off Tebco Terrace in Holgate. That's where my brother and friends rented a house. Post-Labor Day surfs in hurricane swells with a cool offshore breeze holding up the faces and the smell of burning leaves somewhere on the mainland— a unique sensory touch. I thank God for the opportunities presented to me on that island and the people that I met there.*

Bruce Saunders is known to most locals as **"HUCKLEBERRY."** It's a name that stuck from being a childhood toe-head with cut-off pants and no shoes. He was introduced to Koseff's Surf Shop by their generous business offer to subtract the amount spent in surfboard rentals from the price of a new Greg Noll surfboard. Huckleberry had his new board, paid in full, by the end of his first summer surfing.

The Saunders family permanently moved from Teaneck to Long Beach Island in 1957 when Huckleberry was nine years old. Huck started surfing when he was fifteen, sharing a friend's board on Leeward Avenue. About the same time, Huck and some friends spotted old surfboards securely stowed under the porch of a Beach Haven Victorian home. These boards were solid redwood with a balsa stringer. Weighing upwards of a hundred pounds, in what could have been a scene from a Mark Twain story, it took two of them, struggling, to get it down to the beach. Without a fin, these boards were impossible to turn. These "borrowed" treasures were always safely returned in time for the weekend arrival of their owners.

Huckleberry's athleticism and passion for the sport, made him a top competitor for the Koseff Team. Huck admits that whenever he could go surfing, he did. In addition to his commitment to surfing, Huck was a gifted high school athlete at Southern Regional High School. Admittedly small for football, he held his own. But, where he really excelled, was on the wrestling mat.

Huckleberry was a four-year varsity letter winner and never lost a high school dual meet except for his very first one. He was driven by the inspiration of his older brother who introduced him to wrestling, but who passed away from leukemia. Huck completed what his brother had started, and was a state wrestling finalist.

After Huck finished college, he spent two winters in California. He lived in the Santa Barbara area including the college town of Isla Vista. This was strategically located near surfing hot spots like Campus Point and El Cap. He made ends meet working for a roofing company that got most of its referrals after it rained and people realized that they had a leak. Keep in mind that it doesn't rain much in Southern California. When it did, it often meant that a sizable front had come through and that there was also surf to be had. If the job entailed driving passed Ventura Pier, and seeing the waves breaking over the pier, Huck often rechecked his cash situation. If he could financially swing it, he turned his van toward the beach and postponed work for another day.

Huck remembers that it wasn't all that crowded in California when he was there in the 1970s. He recalls surfing in Malibu with only about eight people. "Maybe it was because of the war. Guys were in Vietnam or it just wasn't a priority for most people."

Surfing has always remained an integral part of Huck's life. He has taken trips to Hawaii, Costa Rico, Puerto Rico and the Caribbean. One of his favorite breaks is 'Tropicana' in Barbados. Located in front of the Tropicana Hotel, "It's a goofy-footer's dream with lefts that break like Pipeline." The trade-off is that it breaks in about two feet of water with fire coral below. On a recent trip to Puerto Rico, Huck caught up with former teammates from the Koseff Team— Dean Ward and Brian Doll who were there surfing with their sons.

With a grin from ear to ear, Huck talks about surfing with his son, Neil, who is twenty-eight years old. "It's pretty cool how you go out in the water and the next thing you know, your son is with you. Being able to surf with your kid is just the ultimate."

Neil is an accomplished surfer himself. He has surfed all over the world including places as far away as New Zealand and Australia. Neil is passionate about the longboarding experience and recently completed a video compilation of "all East Coast, all longboards," entitled *Drenched in Devotion*. The film premiered at the Long Beach Island Foundation of the Arts and Sciences during the Summer of 2001.

In an interview for that video, Huck talks about East Coast surfers doing well when they travel. "You have to have some kind of knowledge to survive in big surf and we seem to have survived pretty well. There is a common knowledge about the water and the currents—you know how to handle yourself in the water, wherever it is. I can't say it helps my work. A lot of times when I should be working, I'm surfing."

Huck has never forgotten hearing someone say, "Everyday you surf is like adding a day to your life." Huck definitely took that statement to heart. "Luckily I work for myself and I can get away with it most of the time."

> *In your overall life you'd like to see the ocean stay the same, less pollution. You're out there in the water all the time. We're creating our own problems on earth. We're the only ones that can really help. It's time for everybody to look at it strongly and feel that they can do something about it."* - from *Drenched in Devotion* (2001).

DICK CROSTA is a lifelong resident of Beach Haven who recently retired as supervisor of the Beach Haven Public Works Department. Prior to that, he led the Koseff Surf Team as one of the captains. He and his partner in crime, **MICKEY KING**, remember when it was a regular occurrence for the police to curtail surfers access to the ocean during non-surfing hours. If you did happen to get out in the water, the police often waded out to their waist, in hopes of confiscating the board after a wipe out. These were high stakes, especially during the days before leashes. On one occasion, a group of surfers by-passed the beach all together and used a boat to get out to the line-up. The Crosta garvey was strategically anchored off Leeward Avenue, just beyond the breakers. The police begrudgingly waited that day for someone to loose their surfboard . . . but it never happened. That day, the whole group made a clean get-away.

References:

"Competition Wrap Up." *Competition Surf,* (Winter 1966): 40.

"Surf City: Long Beach Island Surfing Championships." *Competition Surf,* (Spring 1966): 36-41.

Drenched in Devotion. A Garage Conspiracy Production/Neil Saunders (2001). Videocassette—Available at local surf shops

(**A**) Sam Baugh making Crashboat, Puerto Rico look easy. This picture was featured in *International Surfing* magazine, June 1965. (**B**) Huckleberry surfing Tropicanna in Barbados, 1973. He's on an 8' gun glassed by Dean Ward. (**C**) Former team captain, Dick Crosta, sporting Koseff-Greg Noll Surf Team jacket, 2002 (**D**) Dean Ward and (**E**) Barbara Oughton at the LBI Surfing Championships, 1965. These pictures appeared in *Competition Surf* magazine, Spring 1966.

(F) The Koseff-Greg Noll Surfing Team after a successful day at the LBI Surfing Championships held in Surf City on Sept. 11, 1965; This photo appeared in *Competition Surf*, Spring 1966. Standing from left: Ernest Koseff (sponsor), Dean Ward (1st Men), Dave Shinn (3rd Men), Barbara Oughton 1st Women), Jill Anderson (3rd Women), Renny Koseff (sponsor). Kneeling from left: Mark Sellarole (3rd Jr. Men), Bruce "Huckleberry" Saunders (2nd Jr. Men), Bob Spiegle (1st Jr. Men). (G) Ernest Koseff poses with Bonnie "Hazel Hotcurl"

Roth in front of the infamous Koseff Surf Team van. (H) Huckleberry stylin' at the LBI Surfing Championship; *Competition Surf*, Spring 1966. (I) Mark Sellarole on the inside as Sam Baugh works the outside at the LBI Open held on Nelson Avenue in Beach Haven, Sept. 10, 1966. Picture featured in *Competition Surf*, Winter 1966. (J) Barb Oughton and Joey (Rohrer) Adric at the LBI Surfing Championship, 1965 - Featured in *Competition Surf*, Spring 1966. Joey, was inducted into the East Coast Legends Hall of Fame in 1998, but Barb was talented enough to beat her during this event.

WALTERS SURF SHOP

In 1965, Robert and Margaret Walters started their summer business on 5th and the Boulevard in Ship Bottom. They offered a complete shop for bicycles—rentals, sales, and repairs. They also rented everything imaginable, from umbrellas, chairs, and rafts, to televisions and toasters.

Margaret admits that they didn't know a thing about surfboards at the time, but Robert thought it might have potential in their mom and pop store. He placed an order for a hundred Surf Tiger pop-out surfboards from a New York manufacturer. Reportedly, the man taking the order just about fell over when he got that call. He didn't have the ability to produce that volume of boards for one summer and the Walters soon found they didn't want him to. Every Surf Tiger they owned eventually delaminated, with the noses peeling off. It gave plenty of repair business to Ron Jon Surf Shop just a few blocks away.

Initially, surfboard sales and rentals were conducted from the back of the building, in a section called WEB (**W**alters **E**quipment for the **B**each). Surf Tiger was replaced by California-made boards like G&S and Con. Walters Surf Shop was one of the first businesses to sponsor an actual surf team, although it only lasted one season. On one occasion, team members Bobby Jensen and Alan Lee accompanied Robert Walters for a promotional presentation about surfing at a school in Cranford. Jensen remembers surfing with Claude Codgen in Holgate during one of his trips to Ship Bottom to promote his signature series Con boards.

Robert Walters worked year-round as an instrument mechanic for Merck Pharmaceuticals in Rahway. Margaret kept the business going until Robert returned on the weekends and during his four week vacations. In the winter, they sold surfboards out of their basement in Cranford. Oldest son Bill Walters ran a surfboard and bike rental business in Barnegat Light on Broadway and 6th Street in 1969. The family eventually got out of the surfing trade completely in 1987 to focus completely on their bicycle business.

Walters Bicycle Shop is still in existence at the same location, and is operated by Margaret and her son, Tom. Margaret is proud that Robert always ran a reputable business. "Even little kids would bike all the way from Beach Haven to see us because they knew we were honest." Regretably, Robert Walters passed away five years ago. His legacy and his contribution to LBI surfing lives on.

Walters Surf Shop in Ship Bottom—Logos and store, circa 1966

The best summer **Bobby Jensen** ever had may have been the Summer of 1966. That's when he worked for John Maschal at Gourmet's Mooring. He worked from 6 P.M. to 6 A.M., starting out as a dishwasher, and eventually becoming a baker at the Crust & Crumb. From 7 A.M. to 10 A.M. he hit the surf on his beach. Then it was off to a surfing beach for another two hours. That left Bobby plenty of time to grab something to eat, sleep, and do it all over again.

There wasn't much that Bobby wouldn't do to get in the water. He remembers hitchhiking the eighty miles from Roselle Park to LBI with his friend Greg Burnett. Greg's grandmother had a house on the island. If sleeping accommodations were ever a problem, they knew that they could always get into her garage and sleep in the Lincoln Continental that was parked there.

Bobby joined the Navy in 1967 and worked as an oceanographer. After stints in Alaska and Key West, he was stationed in Hawaii. He has lived in Hawaii ever since 1969. Bobby took classes at the University of Hawaii for an amazing twelve years. According to Bobby, he wanted to "maximize his surfing time." Anticipating that the math and science fields would be too demanding and conflict with his surfing, he worked on bachelor and masters degrees in Eastern Philosophy. Not only did Bobby's essay writing improve - so did his surfing.

Bobby also received a masters degree in educational technology. That opened the door for him to work initially with Hawaiian Public Television. Since then, Bobby has been working as a videographer for Boeing. Bobby was also affiliated with the *Surf News Network* for fourteen years. This network provided morning surf reports and afternoon updates to as many as a dozen radio stations throughout the Hawaiian Islands.

Bobby is respected in the surfing community for his growing collection of magazines, posters, and memorabilia. He helped to organize a vintage surf auction and also loaned memorabilia to several Hawaiian museums. He was one of the editors for the *Surfing Collectibles Guide: Magazine & Poster Issue, 2000*. Anyone interested in this very informative guide can contact the publisher in Hawaii at 808)335-2701 or *delavega@lava.net*.

Bobby's passion for wave riding helped him achieve national level status in body boarding competition from 1977 to 1987. Wave riding is still part of Bobby's typical day. At fifty-five years old, he still enjoys "surfing an hour or so everyday before work" and looks forward to having his eight-year-old son out in the lineup with him soon.

ACUFF SURF SHOP

In 1963, another shop at the southern end of Long Beach Island was **Acuff Surf Shop**, owned and operated by brothers Frank and Mark Acuff. It was located on the corner of 15th Street and Bay Avenue in North Beach Haven. It was well known to Chuck Barfoot since it was situated close to his childhood home on West 16th Street. We'll let Chuck tell the rest of the story . . .

> *I was eleven years old at the time. I remember going up to the beach and seeing one of them (Acuff) surfing. I was instantly hooked and wanted to surf. At this time, I had never seen or heard of surfing but knew that I just had to surf!*
>
> *I went to the surf shop and Frank Acuff took an instant liking to me. He just happened to have a beat up 8'6" Dewey Weber. It was a classic wide square tail with a monster multiple wood laminated fin. I just had to have it! He offered it to me for $50. That was a lot of money at the time but I didn't care. My mom and dad told me they would match the money that I earned cutting lawns. After a couple of weeks I was able to come up with the money . . . best money I ever spent."*

The second I got it, Frank helped me wax it up with paraffin and I was off to the beach. It was early June. The water was freezing and the waves were 2' lappers off the south side of the 15th Street jetty. I don't recall seeing anyone else on the beach. I jumped in, paddled out, and caught my first wave. I stood up all the way to the beach and just flipped out. I stayed out until I was blue and couldn't stay a minute longer.

From that time and for the next year, Frank would pick me up in his old monster convertible Buick with the AM radio blasting. My mom would just shake her head. It was totally classic. He would show up in my driveway and just beep the horn. I'd run out the door with my board and throw it in nose first behind the front seat with the tail sticking straight up in the air.

Frank built my second surfboard. It was an 8'10" with a pivot fin. He made my fin out of some left over scrap and it happened to work really well for me. The shape was similar to the Weber hatchet fin that came out a couple of years later on the Weber Performers.

I lost track of Frank and Mark the next year. Through the grapevine I heard Frank was having (health) problems and being so young, I did not understand. It's a shame I never got to thank him for all he had done. Hopefully he knew.

BRANT BEACH SURF SHOP—Richard Lisiewski

Lots of teenagers see pictures in magazines of something they would like to try. For most, this is just a passing fad. For others, like Richard Lisiewski, it would become a way of life.

Rich was about fourteen when he saw an article about Hawaiian surfing in *Life Magazine*. In the 1940s, living sixty miles from the nearest beach, and in New Jersey no less, the chances of finding a surfboard were slim to none. The logical thing to do was to build one, based on pictures from the magazine. A friend of the family who built cabinets for Chris Craft boats agreed to help. The result was a 15' board made of exterior plywood with balsa ribs, weighing upwards of 55 pounds. It had brass fittings at both ends to drain the water.

Rich's first surfing safari was to Seaside. It became evident that day that 15' of board was a lot to handle. If Rich was green at building surfboards, he wasn't much better at the prototype for car racks either. Returning from that first surf session, the board, thought to be secured to the top of the car, flew off and was run over by a truck. It was back to the drawing board.

The next surfboard is one that Rich proudly displays until this day. The ends were made rounder and the height and weight were modestly decreased to ten feet and about forty pounds. This board was first paddled in the Delaware River to make sure it was seaworthy.

Rich spent many summers using it while vacationing at his parents' summer home in Beach Haven in the 1940s. He later used it at Montauk Point, New York when he was stationed in the Army there from 1951 to 1953. In all that time, he never encountered another surfer in the water. Richard says he found out much later that someone named Stretch Pohl had been building boards in Ship Bottom. Unfortunately, he didn't know it at the time and never met him.

Rich recounts some of the early tribulations he encountered. When he built his first board, he didn't know anything about using a fin to improve maneuverability. Another basic accessory that he didn't have was surfboard wax. Tired of slipping on the board, Rich cut inner tubes into bands and then stretched several of them width wise around the board. It actually did the job.

When Rich's family business (hotel and restaurant) in Riverside, New Jersey was sold in 1962, his interest in surfing took a new turn. Back on LBI, surfing's popularity was increasing. Rich thought there might be a business opportunity in beach wholesale products.

Rich enlisted the help of a friend, Frank Collier, who was an expert woodworker. In the Hapico Woodworking Factory in Riverside, Frank and Rich began mass production of wooden skateboards and skimboards. By the 1960's, wood surfboards were all but obsolete. Rich now had to learn to work with polyurethane foam.

As luck would have it, Rich found former surfboard shaper, Jimmy Hine. Jimmy was a California native stationed in the Army at Fort Monmouth, New Jersey. Jimmy, who had worked for Con Surfboards, was happy to share what he knew about the art of building surfboards in return for some off-base travel, home-cooked meals, and surfing conversation.

With this new information in hand, Rich began experimenting in his mother's basement. He later got some help regarding different resins from Charlie Foss who still owns and operates Foss Foam in California. "It was all trial and error back then. At first, we only knew about boating resins. We had a hard time getting things to cure the right way. We definitely didn't know anything about using masks or ventilation like they do today." Even though the boards were getting better, they still had a long way to go. Rich's mother suggested going to California to "learn the right way."

In 1965, Rich and Frank spent three months in Costsa Mesa, California. They worked for Bob Bollen who manufactured "The Greek" line of boards. You may remember names like *Eliminator*, *Liquidator*, and *Aficianado* which are prized by collectors today. While in California, Rich and Frank learned about catalyst to resin ratios and temperature control for resin curing. They also refined their sanding techniques.

In true surfer fashion, Bob Bollen took off for the coast for a week while the surf was up. This left Rich and Frank the run of the mill. They used this to their advantage and did as much snooping as they could. Rich and Frank got the names and addresses of all the product manufacturers they would need to mass produce their own surfboards. Their mission was complete - equipped with valuable information and experience, they headed back to the East Coast to start production.

Rich's big break came when he exhibited his boards at the Boat Show in the New York Coliseum in January 1966. That exposure moved his surfboard building into full swing. That is, until neighboring tenants at the factory complex started to complain that they were getting ill from the resin smell. Rich attempted to disguise the smell with commercial air fresheners, but to no avail. The building custodian was forced to move them to another site where they lasted for another two months before being permanently shut down. Rich filled as many of the pre-existing orders as he could, often working from the basements of family members before he closed down.

All in all, Rich built approximately 3,000 belly boards, wake boards, rescue paddle boards, and surfboards. He manufactured a custom *Collier* and also a pop-out *Matador*. Rich was unique in that instead of relying on outside vendors to supply the surfboard foam "blank," he even learned to "blow his own foam" using 9'8" and 10' fiberglass molds.

No longer able to build surfboards, Rich decided to try his hand at retail. Just in time for the 1966 summer season, Rich rented a storefront on 34th and Bay Avenue in Brant Beach and opened as the Brant Beach Surf Shop. In those early days, the hot items were Mexican blankets, Baja jackets, water buffalo sandals, and huraches. He was one of the first people on the island to sell bikinis, already gaining popularity in California, but still new enough in New Jersey to raise some eyebrows. Rich carried over-run and irregular surfing baggies for four dollars. At that time, surfboard wax was sold to retailers in ten pound blocks. Stores then cut them into one pound pieces, getting about fifty cents per pound or three dollars for the whole ten pound block.

Through the 1970s, the surf shop grew to carry a wide range of beach items, tee shirts, and rental products. Rich had a thriving business until, as fate would have it, he was again forced to move. This time, the building's owner, the Colony Theatre, was expanding and needed more floor space. The doors of Brant Beach Surf Shop permanently closed November 1980.

In 1982, Brighton Beach Surf Shop opened its doors on 86th Street and the Boulevard, continuing the rental and sales business where it left off. The business has always been exclusively a mom and pop store. Rich's wife, Pauline, has been providing assistance with the retail business since the very beginning. Rich also gets some help from his son, Michael. It's hard to tell who gets more pride telling the stories of surfing eras gone by. All the stories are backed-up by a growing collection of surfboards, magazines, and memorabilia from every decade of surfing since the 1940s.

(**Top**) Richard Lisiewski working at his surfboard factory in 1965, putting the finishing touches on a 'competition band.' (**Bottom Left**) Richard and his wife Pauline standing on the beach in Holgate, circa 1952. He is holding the wooden surfboard that he built. (**Bottom Right**) Richard and Pauline have made a life around surfing. In 2003 they still own and operate Brighton Beach Surf Shop.

RICK SURF SHOP—Jim Fitz-Randolph

If given the opportunity to manage a surf shop on LBI or work in North Jersey as a seasonal employee in a factory, which would you take? The choice was pretty obvious for Jim Fitz-Randolph or "Fitz", as most people have known him.

Fitz, a Piscataway native, had been surfing since he was in high school. In 1966, while buying a board at Custom Surf Shop in Lavalette, he unassumingly found himself talking to the shop's owner Joe "Simmo" Simmonella. Simmo had a number of surf shops and was looking for people to help manage them. Fitz, a junior on summer break from Rutgers University, jumped at the chance to spend the summer at the beach. The shop was located on Barnegat Avenue and the Causeway in Ship Bottom. Today, it's the site of Eckerd Drugs. Back then it was a small strip mall with Custom Surf Shop on the north side, followed by a dry cleaning store, and a deli.

Fitz admits that the shop wasn't too much to look at. Unfortunately, it offered even less in terms of living accommodations. Behind a wall in the back of the store was a bathroom and just enough room to sleep. The kitchen was a refrigerator and a hot plate. Hot showers were made possible by Steve Jones' family who lived down the street. Fitz's personal telephone was a pay phone inside the store. And who needs a rolodex when you can just write phone numbers on the wall? That system worked well until the year the walls were repainted.

In 1967, Fitz was given the opportunity to assume the lease of the shop and to buy out Simmo's LBI inventory. That year, he changed the name to Rick Surf Shop which it remained until 1973. The inventory included surfing clothing and accessories, and Rick Surfboards out of Hermosa Beach, California.

Fitz decided to save on freight by transporting whatever surfboards could fit in and on his van. Sometimes that meant surfboard racks with eight to ten boards on top. The trip became a regular sojourn as Fitz traveled back and forth to graduate school in chemical engineering at UCLA. These cross-country adventures always got some "looks" from the middle of the country where people weren't accustomed to long hair and beach clothes, let alone surfboards. One of Fitz's cross-country trips especially paid off in 1968, when, in the middle of the summer season, the trend in surfboard design abruptly changed. Advertisements and articles in surfing magazines were extolling the benefits of a much shorter configuration. Almost overnight, longboards had become outdated.

Most business owners in the East had stocked their inventories pre-season with longboards. They didn't have the capital or connections to get a quantity of these new shortboards in their inventory before the end of the season. Fitz, on the other hand, never had any capital to speak of. It was natural for him throughout the summer to nearly sell out of boards and rely on that income to buy the next batch. His timely "next batch" were the shortboards that everyone was reading about but had never seen. Meanwhile, many of the other surf shops found themselves overstocked with longboard inventory that they couldn't sell.

Bill Willem was one of the team riders for Rick Surf Shop. He remembers the year that Fitz came back from California with his vanload of "short" 7' surfboards. "Fitz was really the one who brought shortboards to the island for the first time and turned us on to them." Bill and his teammates on the Rick Team took to the new shortboards quickly. He recalls that he and Chip Hunt (now working as a geologist in Diamond Head, Hawaii) and Bill Thomas, took turns winning the Labor Day LBI Surfing Competition for three years after shortboards were introduced.

Fitz's close connections with California kept him on the cutting edge of new surfing trends. When it came to the business, Fitz readily admits, "In retrospect, that business wasn't run very well. A Koseff's or a Ron Jon's, obviously knew what they were doing in the business world. They had some experience from their family businesses and it showed. I was still learning on the job."

Nevertheless, Fitz wasn't afraid to explore other business opportunities and learn from his mistakes. He owned other surf shops in Lavalette and Cocoa Beach, Florida. At one point, he was importing flip flops from Taiwan, which he also wholesaled to other surf shops. A little bit less successful was a take-off of the Kanvas by Katin board short that was also made overseas. All the shorts were returned when the salt water corroded the eyelets and snaps on this product. Fitz also dealt with secondhand clothing. One of the bales he received included a whole shipment of tuxedos. It made for an interesting surf shop advertisement: *Free tuxedo with every purchase.*

Fitz eventually built a warehouse on the mainland in West Creek in an effort to expand his import business of sandals. After Fitz closed the surf shop business in 1974, the building became the home of Handmade Furniture Company which it has been ever since. Fitz drew on his knowledge of working with resins and began applying them to furniture, on the order of the hatchcover phenomenon. He found that the custom woodworking business has provided more of a stable constant in his life compared to the seasonal trends of the surfing industry.

Don't worry, Fitz never left the surfing world. At fifty-seven, he lives in Loveladies and gets to make the decision every morning if he wants to surf or go to work. He has surfed all over the world, Hawaii, Central and South America, and the South Pacific. Fitz is grateful for improved surfing equipment. He still remembers the stiff Parkway diving suits that you would "somehow get on and off and the boots and gloves that were then duck taped on." Frozen hair was part of the deal. The second-hand army trench coats sold at Rick Surf Shop came in handy *trying* to warm-up afterwards.

Fitz nostalgically remembers the days when any surfer who needed a place to stay was always welcome to a spot on the floor in his surf shop overnight. Sometimes that meant waking people up in the morning in order to maneuver the boards to their outside display. Temporary housing for surfers was also made possible by boats which were supposed to be in winter storage in the parking lot close-by. Locals remember the shop as "nothing flashy" and a "hard core" surf shop. Fitz was "hard core" before the term ever existed.

Advertisement for Rick Surf Shop which appeared in *The Beachcomber*, August 23, 1973, page 11.

CHITO'S SURF SHOP—Walter Chito Gebhart

The northern end of Long Beach Island has always been more residential than commercial. Despite a strong following of surfers from this end, surf shops located north of the Causeway have always been relatively scarce. Chito's Surf Shop made its mark, with several locations from Ship Bottom to Barnegat Light from 1969 to 1976.

Walter Chito (Latin family name) Gebhart was familiar with the Barnegat Light area. Originally from Philadelphia, his family bought a summer home in Barnegat Light in 1956. The house was rebuilt after it was destroyed in the Storm of 1962. Chito started surfing in 1965 when he was sixteen years old.

From 1967 to 1971, while attending the University of Pennsylvania's Wharton Business School, Chito decided to take a stab at the surf shop business. He opened a shop on Broadway Avenue (the fork off the Boulevard) in Barnegat Light in 1969. He was there one year, carrying the California-based line of Petrillo surfboards. In 1970, he moved the store location to 24th Street and the Boulevard in Ship Bottom. He expanded his product line to include some wetsuits, Kanvas by Katin board shorts, and El Paipo knee machines.

Chito used his month-long break from school every January to drive to California to do his buying for the summer business. During his second trip, he stayed with Petrillo's factory manager and learned all he could about building surfboards. When he finished college in 1971, he drove to California with a rented U-Haul to bring back surfboard blanks, a five hundred pound drum of resin, and bolts of fiberglass cloth.

His third year in business, Chito began building and selling his own line of surfboards exclusively. He moved back to Barnegat Light again, this time to one of the fisherman's sheds that is now in Viking Village. The logo for the Chito Surfboard was a skeleton key. He advertised the board as, "The key that will open up the green room." In all, Chito built about three hundred surfboards. He also remembers accommodating several individuals by removing and then reshaping the noses of their personal longboards. This was done in an effort to keep up with the short board revolution. Most of Chito's boards were in the seven-foot range. Chito's skills progressed to allow him to design boards with channel bottoms and also try other experimental designs. Chito's final location was a rented storefront that was part of the Harvey Cedars Marina complex. He was there from 1973 to 1976. The retail business was located in the front of the building. Shaping and glassing took place in a room in the back. It's been rumored that it took two years before the next tenants stopped smelling the resin.

In the off-season of the early 1970s, Chito helped make ends meet by delivering boats up and down the East Coast. He remembers one trans-Atlantic trip that should have taken seventeen days. The unpredictable weather patterns during late autumn turned it into a sixty-three day trip that is a "story in itself." In 1974, Chito spent October through May refurbishing a twenty-nine foot sailboat that he then took to the Bahamas with some very important cargo—surfboards.

When Chito decided to get out of the surfboard business in 1976, it was a natural transition to get into the boat industry. In the fall of that year, he moved to California and worked for a company that made tooling for boat parts. He then went on board with Lancer Yacht Company (now defunct) as a service representative and eventually their chief engineer. Today he owns his own boat service business in San Juan Capistrano, California, specializing in marine electronics. He is also a feature writer for boating magazines.

Chito was a competitive soccer player in college and returned to the sport when he moved to California. He is presently coaching an elite women's team that is ranked fifth in the country. He admits that his time on the water these days is limited primarily to boating. Brother Andres is still hitting the surf. He is a big wave surfer, living in Carpenteria, California. Andres has been known to surf Rincon at night with a light stick, just to avoid the crowds.

Chito fondly remembers his time on LBI, especially the Septembers when surfing restrictions were lifted and the seasons began to change. He recalls the primitive days of quarter inch dive wetsuits and the best surf always seeming to be when the water was 40°. "That's when you could only stand it for twenty minutes at a time. You'd have to run home, pour hot water down your wetsuit, and go out for another twenty minutes."

Sixties Long Beach Island Surfing Contests

August 8, 1964. Surf City - 75 contestants and 3000 spectators. One of the spectators was surfing legend, Greg Noll. The resulting parking problems caused Surf City officials to insist on a post-Labor Day Contest the following year.

July 31, 1965. Essex Avenue in Harvey Cedars. The event was reported by Stretch Pohl in *Surfing East* (1965). Stretch makes particular mention that, "It should be noted that only Harvey Cedars, under the guidance of Mayor Thomas and the residents, set aside two 'surfing only' beaches." The competition was sponsored by the Long Beach Island Surfing Association (L.B.I.S.A.) for its members exclusively. Sixty individuals competed.

> MEN-1. Raymond Bachtle, 2. Bruce Saunders, 3. Dean Ward
> JUNIOR MEN-1. Bob Spiegle, 2. Gordon Throast, 3. Ken Binder
> WOMEN-1. Joey Rohrer, 2. Barbara Oughton, 3. Jane Lewis

September 11, 1965. Surf City. The competition was sponsored by the L.B.I.S.A. *Surfing East* (1965) and *Competition Surf* (1966) both reported on this event. Two to four foot surf held up for eighteen heats.

MEN-1. Dean Ward, 2. Gary Danielson, 3. Dave Shimm
JUNIOR MEN-1. Bob Spiegle, 2. Bruce Saunders, 3. Mark Sellarole
WOMEN-1. Barbara Oughton, 2. Joey Rohrer, 3. Jill Anderson
OUTSTANDING SURFER AWARD- Dean Ward

September 10, 1966. Nelson Avenue in Beach Haven. *Competition Surf* (1966) reported: Two to three foot waves with a light offshore wind. Heat coordinators : Ralph Bourgeois, Ray Bachtle, Charles Paul. Judges : Gary Philhower, Mark Acuff, Charlie Ackers
Trophies presented by Ralph Bourgeois, President of the L.B.I.S.A. and Beach Haven Mayor Don Rommel

MEN-1. Ray Bachtle, 2. Bruce Saunders, 3. Bill Lammers
JUNIOR MEN-1. Sam Baugh, 2. Bob Spiegle, 3. Ernie Baugh
WOMEN-1. Laura Powers, 2. Cathy Butchko, 3. Ginger Wilson

References:

Bakst, Roger. "Competition Wrap Up: Third Long Beach Island Open Surfing Contest." *Competition Surf* (Winter 1966): 40.

Pohl, Stretch. "Surf-n-Line: New Jersey." *Surfing East* (Autumn 1965): 56.

"Surf City: Long Beach Island Surfing Championships" *Competition Surf* (Spring 1966): 36-41.

"Surf-n-Line." *Surfing East* (Winter 1965): 53.

(A) 1967 Surfing Contest Poster (B) LBI Surfing Championship held in Surf City on September 11,1965. Mayor Bruce Nelson of Surf City, N.J. congratulates the winners from left to right: Bob Spiegle (1st Jr. Men), Bruce Saunders (2nd Jr. Men), Mark Sellarole (3rd Jr. Men), Dean Ward (1st Men and Outstanding Surfer Award), Mayor Nelson, David Shinn (3rd Men), Gary

Danielson (2nd Men), Barbara Oughton (1st Women), Joey Rohrer (2nd Women), Jill Anderson (3rd Women). **(C)** The Judges' Stand during September 1965 Contest: Mike Gordon Hawes, Gibson, Frank Acuff, Ralph Bourgeois, Biff Barrett **(D)** 1964 Surf Contest Poster **(E)** Surf City contest crowd, pictured in *Competition Surf*, Spring 1966.

Ladies of Long Beach Island

Barbara (Oughton) Baptista, a.k.a. "Barb"

Barb Oughton learned to surf on Leeward Avenue during the summer of 1964, thanks to a lesson from Roger Bakst. That single event inspired this seventeen year old young lady to get in the water every day after that, three or four hours a day. First she borrowed boards, and then bought one with her brother. Barb finished second at the LBI Surfing Contest at the end of that first summer. With that, she was invited to join the Koseff Surf Team. Not bad for someone who had only learned to swim three years earlier.

Barb attended Penn State and graduated in 1968. From there she moved to California and performed with a professional water ballet group. She traveled with the ballet group to Japan where she stayed for four months. Barb took advantage of the situation and not only surfed in Japan but Australia and Hawaii as well, when she made her trip back to California.

Barb was hooked on surfing traveling adventures. While attending San Diego State University and working on a masters degree, she made frequent surfing sojourns to Baja, Mexico. She later traveled to France and Spain (Santander & Canary Islands) and Central America. After three years of teaching junior high in Vista, California, Barb left her job to take the trip of her life. She drove a Toyota Land Cruiser through Mexico, Central America, the Pacific Coast of South America, and then up the Atlantic coast of Argentina, Uruguay, and Brazil.

Through a series of plane and bus rides, Barbara then ended up in Florianopolis in Santa Catarina, in the southern part of Brazil. She planned to teach English there long enough to get back on her feet financially. Her plans abruptly changed when she met and later married Mario Baptista. They have lived in Brazil ever since and raised two daughters who are now twenty-one and nineteen years old.

Barb briefly returned to the states in the late 1980s to complete an applied linguistics doctorate degree at UCLA. Barb presently teaches at a university in Brazil. Regretably, Barb stopped surfing in 1990 because of back problems. Unable to separate herself from the water completely, since 1993 she has been very successful in open water swimming competition.

Ironically, at the time of this interview, Barb who is now fifty-five years old had just purchased a funboard. She was hopeful that her back would allow her to start surfing again. "I catch grief regularly from my daughters who think that a woman of my age with back problems has no business trying to surf again." My money is on Barb getting back out there and reliving the stoke. Barb sends her best regards to everyone on LBI.

* * *

Patrica Browning (Lauer) Roth, a.k.a. "Bonnie" or "Hazel Hotcurl"

Bonnie was a summer resident of LBI in her youth, hailing from Bryn Mawr, Pennsylvania. As long as she could remember, she was involved in anything and everything to do with water. Early on, she raced sailboats and later taught sailing. She was a competitive swimmer and worked as a lifeguard. In 1963, when she was twelve years old, she was introduced to surfing and was competing the following year. She eventually earned the nickname, "Hazel Hotcurl" for some of her fancy footwork on a surfboard.

When Bonnie was fourteen years old, she worked for a season at Koseff's Surf Shop. No doubt she gave Koseff's a run for their money the next three summers. That's when this budding entrepreneur opened a surf shop of her own in her family's garage. For the right price, she would rent you one of her three boards: Sears pop-out, Duke, or Greg Noll. She was also happy to oblige with a surf lesson or two.

Bonnie's obsession with surfing was undeniable. She proudly named their family cat Dewey Weber. Bonnie also convinced her mom to store one of her boards in the kitchen. All 9' of it was securely stowed above the length of the kitchen cabinets. Even when Bonnie scribbled, she scribbled surfing. Her surfing cartoons would later be featured in LBI's local newspaper, *The SandPaper* as well as Florida's *Tampa Tribune*. In December 1967, *The Sunday Bulletin (Philadelphia)* ran a whole page story about Bonnie Roth—The Radnor High School junior, who was preparing for the Polar Bear Surfing Contest at the end of the month in Ocean City, New Jersey.

Bonnie's overall water-knowledge helped qualify her for a summer position with the Marine Police when she was eighteen years old. She loved every minute of it. Having a job that was in and around the water was heaven for Bonnie. From the fall through spring, Bonnie attended the University of Tampa, focusing on physical and special education. She has used her degree "here and there" through the years, mainly as a substitute teacher. When a full-time position with the Marine Police became available in 1971, that's where Bonnie went, and stayed, for eleven years in all. She was eventually promoted to Marine Police Sergeant, a position she liked the least because it confined her to a desk. Besides providing information about boating safety, Bonnie was involved in a number of life-threatening situations. She even delivered a baby in the middle of the bay off Harvey Cedars.

Bonnie grew up learning how to clam and also helped her mother operate a small summer clam business. When Bonnie left the Marine Police to spend more time with her family, it was a natural transition to get involved in this business again. As a wholesale seafood distributor and clam broker, Bonnie still operates *Capt. Brownie* in Barnegat.

Bonnie has continued her passion for water sports, just with bigger and faster toys over the years. In the late 1970s, Bonnie raced speed garveys. She then competed with ocean racing boats for eleven years. Both types of boats were named "Kamakaze," a name that Bonnie fell in love with because of its translation, "Divine Wind."

Bonnie knows she is very fortunate that her husband Bob is a "water rat" as well. Fittingly, they were married in the middle of the bay, near Brant Beach Yacht Club. Bonnie still surfs when she gets a chance. She prefers her 7'4" Heritage single fin the most. Her last big surfing excursion was to Hawaii in 1980. Everyone told her she could easily rent a board in Hawaii, but when she got there, it was a different story. Desperate to catch some waves, she finally coaxed a local into letting her borrow a board. The stipulation was that she had to leave her husband for collateral . . . the things you do to be able to surf.

* * *

Mary (Buck) Frack

Mary Buck was from Bucks County, Pennsylvania and a summer resident in Holgate during her childhood. She was eight years old when she first saw someone surfing at the end of her street. At that instant, she knew it was something that she just had to do. Her mother insisted that she was still "too little" to surf. Mary painfully waited until she was eleven years old to get her chance.

At first, Mary had to borrow boards. She would often go up to a group of young surfers who were sitting on the beach and socializing. She would ask if she could borrow a board. The response was often with a snicker, "If you can get it out there, you can have it." Somehow, Mary always got it out there. She readily admits that with her small frame and the size of the boards in 1965, it might take "20 leg circles" to finally get the board turned around toward the beach. She'd miss the first wave in the set and have to wait to catch the next one. Once she was out there, she didn't want to come in. The board's owner would inevitably have to come out to the line-up to get it back from her. Mary saved every penny of her birthday and Christmas money. She worked tirelessly delivering newspapers for two years. When other kids were buying ice cream, Mary was eating apples from her house. All this was done in order to purchase her first surfboard, a 9'3" Ventura. When the summer was over, twelve-year-old Mary insisted that the board come back to Pennsylvania with her. It sat in her bedroom all winter. "It was my pride. I just thought surfing was the coolest thing."

Mary recalls that she and some friends learned to ride a unicycle for the sole purpose of not having to awkwardly hold onto a bike with one hand and a surfboard with the other. Mary surfed diligently but competed minimally through her teens. She was turned off by contests that she felt were poorly judged and by prizes that favored the male competitor. She recalls a first place prize for men being $100 and a wetsuit and first place in the women's category being a wetsuit vest.

When Mary was nineteen, she met Jesse Frack, a local surfboard shaper. "He coached me and really wanted me to be a professional surfer. I told him I wanted him to be a professional musician." Mary was one of several professional musicians in her family. When the two met, Mary was playing bass guitar in a band and also performing solo. At first, Jesse didn't buy into the musician thing and Mary never bought into becoming a professional surfer. Mary loved to surf but was happier surfing when she wanted to, rather than all the conditions encountered in competition.

Besides surfing and music, gymnastics has also been a big part of Mary's life. She has been a competitor and coach since the time she was seventeen years old. She has coached at the recreational, club, and high school levels (Toms River East, Southern Regional). She was selected as "All County Coach of the Year" by the Times Beacon Newspapers in 2002 for her work with Southern Regional High School. Besides Mary's coaching talents, she holds a teaching degree with a physical education emphasis from Trenton State College.

Mary and Jesse Frack married in 1979 and lived in Santa Barbara for six years. That's when Mary got involved again in competitive surfing, this time with the Western Surfing Association (WSA). She can still see the fluid and artistic moves of a young surfer who she frequently surfed with at Hammond's Reef. That surfer was none other than three-time surfing world champion, Tommy Curren. Mary was friends with Curren's mother who was also the head of the Santa Barbara Chapter of the WSA.

During the finals of one of the WSA competitions, Mary remembers doing well but feeling very dizzy on the beach. That was her first indication that she was pregnant. Mary continued surfing up until the fourth month with all of her children, Adam (19), Sara (16), and Dana (14). When Mary couldn't tolerate lying on her abdomen anymore, she simply paddled on her knees whether it was getting out to the lineup or paddling for the wave. Mary says all of her children can stand up on a board. Adam recently came back from a two-week surf trip in California with his dad to visit "Uncle Chucky" Barfoot.

Now forty-eight years old, Mary has continued surfing throughout her life. She has surfed in places like North Carolina, Florida, and Hawaii. She recently participated in a local Pro-Am competition only to find the women's division filled with fifteen-year-old girls. Realizing that her personal surfing experience more than doubled their ages, she petitioned to compete in the men's division. Mary ended up holding her own in a competitive men's heat rather than taking a trophy away from one of the young ladies.

Mary and husband Jesse still surf together. They can also be found performing together musically. Mary got her wish and turned Jesse into a professional musician after all. You can find them on the island performing together at Wida's (*Mary Buck*), as part of a five-piece band at Buckalew's (*Frax Machine*), or in the rhythm section of *Brass Tacks*, a nineteen-piece big band orchestra. They play everything from rock to jazz to blues. They were even invited to play on the Boardwalk outside the Convention Center during the week of pageantry for the Miss America Contest in 2002.

Mary always hoped to make a life out of the three things she loved: music, gymnastics, and surfing. Of these, "The first two paid the bills and surfing has remained my number one outlet and pleasure for all these years."

> *Surfing is an internal spiritual thing. You do it to get in harmony with the wave. Some of the younger kids look like they are trying to destroy the wave instead of working with it. In music, there is a lot of improvisation when performing. You have to improv with the ocean as well— you never know exactly what you're going to get. Like music and like gymnastics, surfing is all about timing.*

* * *

Barbara Conover

Barbara spent her teenage years surfing Normandy Beach, near Seaside, where she grew up. She started surfing with her cousin Ellie when she was fourteen years old. There were no female surfing models at the time, but that didn't stop them. Surfing in the water looked a lot more interesting than just lying on a towel. Barbara was soon surfing Eastern Surfing Association (ESA) contests from New York to North Carolina. When she was twenty-three, Barbara moved to Maui. She spent six months there, working as a waitress, and of course, surfing, every chance she got.

Barbara and her husband moved to Waretown in 1978. That's when she was first introduced to LBI surfing. She's been hitting our waves ever since, while raising three children and working as a permanent substitute teacher at Southern Regional High School (SRHS).

Barbara decided to become more involved with the SRHS Surf Team when her oldest son, Dan, joined the team as a freshman in 1994. At first, she was just judging the meets, but then took on a more active role as an assistant coach. At fifty, Barbara is still coaching and still surfing, and has no intention of stopping either. Out in the water, she prefers her 7'0" or 7'6" funboards. (Check out her picture in the chapter about the SRHS Surf Team). Barbara was thrilled to get out to Hawaii again during the spring of 2002. She was visiting her son, Dan, who is a U.S. Marine stationed in Hawaii. Barbara spent Mother's Day weekend surfing Waikiki and the North Shore. That's one cool mom!

* * *

Barbara Robertson a.k.a. "Magnolia Bulkhead"

Barbara started surfing in 1964 in Seaside Park. She remembers constantly begging rides from anyone who could get her to the waves. When she could finally drive herself, she was up and down the Parkway in search of waves, her 9'6" G&S sticking out of her tiny Triumph TR4. Barbara started hitting the LBI area in 1975. At fifty-two, Barbara has never stopped her wave quest, despite a few snags along the way.

When her son Tim was a baby, and her husband was working double-shifts, Barbara desperately needed to catch a couple of waves. She safely left her son sleeping and nestled in his baby carrier on the beach. One day, three other mothers didn't see it that way and surrounded the carrier with their arms crossed in condemnation. Barbara decided she would have to let the waves wait until another day.

In recent years, "bad knees and back" have been catching up with Barbara. Especially in the winter, she finds it too hard to push up from the surfboard in a 5-4 wetsuit. Rather than give up the waves completely, this empassioned wave enthusiast just rides a boogie board instead. Barbara surfed Puerto Rico in 1990 and also surfed Hawaii this past May, while visiting her son who now lives there. (It's a good thing those mothers saved Tim from a rogue wave or a psychotic seagull when they did!)

Barbara works in the Manahawkin area in graphic design as a commercial illustrator. She readily admits that she has passed up more lucrative professional opportunities in order to stay closer to the beach. "I gave up financial security to be able to roll out of bed and surf. That has always been my goal. I often surf in the morning before going to work. It just means I'll stay later or take work home. You would think that the older I get, this would change, but it still hasn't." A co-worker chimes in, "I don't know if all surfers are like her, but she has a true passion for surfing."

Despite the obvious impression that Barbara has made in her work environment, she says she "tries to be inconspicuous" out in the water. "A good day is if no one points at me and laughs. I'm quite a sight trying to squeeze into my wetsuit these days." Barbara is happy to see that there are more young women locally involved in the surfing scene. For Barbara, surfing has been:

> My religion, my prozac. When I'm fried, that's the only place to be.
> Any wave that I catch OR catches me is a good wave.

Reference:

Burden, Nancy. "Bryn Mawr Girl Finds Surfing Really Cool." *The Sunday Bulletin (Philadelphia)* December 17, 1967: 4. Photos by Charles J. Tinney.

Local Surf Legends

Chuck Barfoot

 Chuck Barfoot began surfing when he was eleven years old. He was introduced to surfing by the Acuff brothers who operated Acuff Surf Shop close to his home in North Beach Haven. It didn't take long before Chuck was recognized as a talented local surfer. One day while surfing on 17th Street, an obvious "non-local" paddled out right next to him. This surfer performed the first floater that Chuck had ever seen in his life. It was then that Chuck realized that the rumors about Johnny Fain coming to LBI were true. A mutual admiration society was immediately formed. Fain invited Chuck back to Koseff's Surf Shop to pick out a board for himself. Fain let him try both his Formula 1 and Formula 2 boards. Since Chuck couldn't decide which one he liked best, he got to keep both of them.
 Chuck often surfed the 12th Street break on the North Beach Haven-Beach Haven border because of the leniency of a sympathetic lifeguard. Since this spot was the last guarded beach in Beach Haven, it was also the final morning inspection stop by the lifeguard lieutenant as he made his way south to north. Everyone knew they had an extra thirty to forty-five minutes until the lieutenant arrived on their beach. Once the lieutenant was spotted, the lifeguard whistle blew. That was the signal to get out of the water "pronto." More than once, the lieutenant was a little suspicious when he noticed a lot of guys with surfboards still on the beach at that hour. Adding to the suspicion was the fact that they were dripping wet. Nevertheless, they pulled it off perfectly

for a whole summer thanks to the support of lifeguard **Joe Piscapo** who most people will recognize from "Saturday Night Live" fame. From 1968 to 1974, Chuck bought materials from Ron Jon Surf Shop and built boards in his father's garage. He produced over one hundred boards that he sold out of his house. His boards didn't have a logo but were either signed with his name and a palm tree or the insignia "Bilbo Baggins," a nickname that Tom Sims and Ray "Raisin" DeFrehn gave him. Until the day Chuck's parents sold that property, his father was still chipping resin droppings off the concrete floor in the garage.

Chuck worked at Atlantis Surf Shop from 1970 to 1971. This shop, owned by Butch Gilligan, carried the Weber line of surfboards like: Weber Ski and Weber Australia. It was at Atlantis Surf Shop that Chuck first met Tom Sims. Tom lived in Haddonfield, New Jersey and was trying to wholesale his brand of surfboards. The two quickly became friends and it wasn't long before Chuck, with his carpentry background, was helping Tom to make the first Sims skateboards out of solid oak.

Sims Skateboards was on its way to international recognition in the skateboarding industry. Chuck continued to work with Tom and became involved with the company's research and development, building prototype skateboards for the top pros on the Sim's Skateboard Team. Tom Sims also expanded his product line to include snowboards. Tom bought the rights to a plastic board that had a skateboard deck and skyhooks. At about this same time, the Burton line of boards was also entering the market.

Chuck kept re-thinking this whole new "snow surfing" concept in his mind, using what he knew about designing and riding surfboards. Already adept at working with resins, Chuck made a mold and made his first snowboard using fiberglass with a foam core. It was revolutionary in that the rubber straps Chuck used allowed the rider to perform in a goofy foot or regular stance.

In 1978, Chuck's prototype board opened up a whole new level of performance. The day it was completed, Chuck jumped in the car and headed to Utah from California. Never having been on a snowboard before, Chuck *surfed* his first run down the hill of snow flawlessly. He continued to experiment with new ideas, incorporating surfboard technology such as fins, camber, and channels. He began production of Barfoot custom snowboards in 1981. For his valuable innovation contributions, Chuck Barfoot was inducted into Transworld's Snowboarding Hall of Fame in 1997.

You can find more product information about Barfoot custom snowboards, longboards, skateboards, and wearables at *www.Barfoot.com*. Make sure you tell him *Surfing LBI* sent you.

Chuck Barfoot can make any wave look good: **(A)** Mean and overhead at Holyoke Avenue in Beach Haven, October, 1972 or **(B)** Small and clean at LaConchita, California, 1990. **(C)** Chuck snowboarding in Canada, 1990. **(D)** Back where it all began on Long Beach Island. Fifteen-year-old Chuck poses with his first custom surfboard built by Frank Acuff.

Ken Smith

Ken Smith was a Surf City resident in 1962, when he spent the entire summer carrying his 9'4" Shark pop-out on his head from 10th Street in Surf City to 8th Street in Ship Bottom. "That's what you do when you don't own a car, and that's where all your friends are." Since 8th Street was an all-day surfing beach, that's what Ken did . . . all day, every day. The board, however, may have had a little too much water time. The whole front quarter of the board eventually broke one day while hanging ten on the nose.

That was the incentive needed to "work for credit" to get a new board at Ron Jon Surf Shop. Ken became a burger flipper for the fast food stand in front of the surf shop. He still remembers the sign: *Happiness is a 19¢ Surf Burger.*

Encouraged by friends, Ken even competed in a few contests. He remembers surfing for the Koseff Team with his Ron Jon surfboard. Following one meet in Ocean City, Ken accidentally lost his prescription glasses while walking on the fishing pier. "Blind as a bat" without them, Ken even considered asking a policeman to help him find his group in order to get back home. Fortunately, someone eventually recognized him and yelled his name. Ken insists that he could always see well enough to surf, just not always well enough to find his blanket on the beach if he drifted. More recently, and fortunately for all of us, Ken discovered that eyeglass bands exist for securing glasses out in the water.

For Ken, surfing was "beyond being a sport." Ken explained it this way: "It is you and the God-wonderful ocean, just so natural to be there. And when you get good—cutting the wave and getting in the tube, it takes it to an entirely new level." By August 1966, Ken was ready for new adventures. He set out for the West Coast with $120. Ken surfed Malibu, Seal Beach, Huntington Beach (don't worry, he didn't try to shoot the pier), Doheny, and K38 in Mexico.

Ken's career as a real estate broker allowed him some latitude to get in the water when the surf was up. His career also led him in another direction that he had never planned. Ken found himself investigating and trying to influence legislation effecting beach communities.

It all began when the *Dune and Shorefront Protection Act* was introduced in March 1980. Backed by the Department of Environmental Protection (DEP), this act stated that if one's home was between the ocean and the first parallel paved road, it could not be rebuilt if it were damaged greater than fifty percent. The ramifications of this legislation would be very costly to private homeowners and businesses alike. Ken realized that swift action had to be taken. He became active with Citizens for Local & Intelligent Control (CLIC), originally formed in Ocean City but with chapters in Seaside and on Long Beach Island. Thirty-five-thousand notices were sent to property owners at their primary residences. This was essential for reaching legislators outside of the immediate area. Public outcry was overwhelming and the act was reversed.

The event made Ken realize the importance of being proactive to MAINTAIN beaches and not just react after the fact. With this in mind, Ken became active in the American Shore and Beach Preservation Association (ASBPA) which has been in existence since 1926. The group consists of coastal engineers, geologists, and some legislators who recognize the importance of applying technology to restore beaches. Ken was instrumental, along with Mike O'Brien (Former Dean at Cal-Berkeley) in organizing the N.J. Chapter of ASBPA. Ken has been on its board for twenty years.

Ken's association with ASBPA led him to the further realization that "all the good science in the world didn't mean a thing without the needed political support to carry out recommendations." Ken saw the need for politicking and came up with the idea for *The Coastal Advocate* in 1991. Today, it is a registered lobbying firm in Washington, D.C. and in Trenton. The firm tracks legislation, testifies on coastal bills, and contacts state and federal legislators to promote bills which protect the coast. The Coastal Advocate was instrumental in helping New Jersey become the first state to have an actual "State Shore Protection Fund" utilizing monies from the realty transfer fee.

Ken's commitment to coastal issues took another turn in the late 1980s when the New Jersey coast was inundated with trash, medical waste, and sludge. Ken remembers the devastating effect as bookings were cancelled and the local economy lost an estimated $3 billion in revenue in the 1987 and 1988 seasons. The first public outcry was "Hands Across the Beach," a symbolic gesture promoted by Karen Kiss who soon after became the first president of the Alliance for a Living Ocean (ALO). Ken joined Karen as part of the core group of ALO, a non-profit corporation dedicated to maintaining a healthy coastal environment.

Some of ALO's initial agenda addressed problems associated with the Ciba-Geigy Company pumping residual water from their chemical processes directly into the Atlantic Ocean. The group also made significant headway when it came to the Fresh Kills landfill. Barged trash from New York City's five boroughs is carried to this landfill in Staten Island, N.Y. While the barges got there, in the absence of guard rails and other protective measures, the trash often fell off into the ocean and found its way to New Jersey beaches. Thanks to the successful resolution of both of these issues, the Atlantic Ocean is cleaner than it's been in years.

Ken has remained active in ALO and is proud that the organization didn't dissolve when the trash stopped floating in. He points out that there are constantly new threats to our fragile marine ecosystem. Ken gives a lot of credit to Joan Koons, ALO's president from 1992-2000, who then led the group proactively.

Beginning with Joan, ALO instituted a number of educational programs, many of these for school-age children in order to raise environmental-consciousness and foster good habits. ALO has continued to testify on behalf of the environment at public hearings and maintains communication with all levels of policy makers. ALO also sponsors public events like "The Wave," beach clean-ups, and the adopt-a-storm drain program. Their Marine Debris Sampling Team, which just celebrated its tenth year, was the first in the nation of its kind. Their work set a national standard with an amazing 130 marine debris monitoring sites now in place. These sites are located on the Atlantic, Pacific, and Gulf of Mexico coastlines of the continental U.S., as well as coastlines along Alaska, Hawaii, Puerto Rico, and the U.S. Virgin Islands.

Ken is very proud of ALO's work and encourages anyone interested in protecting our marine environment to find their niche in this volunteer organization. For individuals and businesses who don't have the time to attend all the hearings and conferences regarding local coastal issues, there is The Coastal Advocate. For more information on Coastal Advocate Inc., check out the website at *www.coastaladvocate.com*.

Tom Luker

Tom Luker grew up in the suburbs of Levittown, Pennsylvania. He was a competitive high school swimmer and also an avid body surfer when his family vacationed on the Jersey shore. An a cappella singer himself, he remembers falling in love with the harmony of the Beach Boys music long before he knew what surfing was all about.

He finally got his chance to try surfing in 1965. He and some classmates from Trenton Junior College (known today as Mercer County College) would go to the beaches in the Belmar area. After that, he used every excuse he had to visit his grandparents who owned Farley Grocery Store (presently Reynold's Garden Center) on Bay Avenue in Manahawkin. That made it convenient to surf on LBI, which Tom did as often as he could, until he joined the U.S. Marine Corps.

Tom was stationed in Vietnam from 1969 to 1970. He was given a choice between two assignments and chose the one in Chu Lai, mainly because he learned there were official bathing beaches there. These beaches were staffed with lifeguards who allowed him to surf whenever he desired. Tom even used his surfboard on several occasions, to help with water rescues when, "A soldier from Iowa found himself a little out of his element in the water."

As an airway technician, Tom chose the night shift. That allowed him plenty of time to surf during the day. Shortly after he arrived, he commandeered a board from an Army captain who was being transferred. He remembers getting a copy of *Surfer* magazine and reading about boards being made that were 7' long. "No way," he thought. He had to try a board that size for himself. He made two boards while he was there, scrounging up wood and also using rocket packing foam.

One of Tom's most unique surfing experiences occurred shortly after he met Army Corporal Sammy. Here's the rest of that story in Tom's words :

> *Sammy drove a mail truck and in passing my hooch (six to eight-man tin roofed living quarters) spots my board leaning against the wall. He slams on the breaks and comes screaming, 'who owns the board?' Sammy was from California and couldn't believe there were surfboards in Nam. We hooked up and traded stories. He's also freaking that I'm from the East Coast and am a full-on surfer.*

> *But, the real story to our meeting was a trip that we took two miles up the coast, which lay between the Chu Lai airbase and a Navy river boat unit. Between the two was a no man's land... not ours, not theirs. Sammy tells me about this cove that peels right and peels left, and only breaks when it's over six foot. Sammy makes sure that I'll go.*

> *We got our chance about three weeks later when a nor'easter, just like LBI, came through. Sammy comes by, all freaked out because he drove by the break on the way down, 'Man, the surf is firing today.' We're off in Sammy's vehicle with two M16's, ammo, flack jackets, helmets, and my 10'2" Surfboards Makaha. We bust through the jungle and come out on the rim of the cove about an eighth of a mile across and half that distance out from the rocky beach. Sammy was right. Almost dead center of the cove, they were peeling left and right into a deep trench that made them short and steep with an easy paddle out. They were eight to ten foot on the faces. In that moment, the whole scene was surreal.*

Who goes first? Sammy was the first one to find the place, so he had first dibs. This is not your typical day at the beach. Like I said, we weren't sure who was around . . . us or them. Like myself, Sammy had his baggies under his jungle fatigues. In no time, he was down the twenty-foot drop to the beach and was heading for the line up. We decided on a six wave session each, while the other person stood guard.

On Sammy's first wave, he went right, fading through the bottom turn, into a nice barrel section, out to the shoulder, back down and up over the top for another. I remember hooting like a banshee and waving my M16 around like that was normal.

I got my chance and couldn't help thinking on the paddle out, how bazaar this whole thing was . . . how dangerous, how crazy. As I pulled into the line up and the first set approached, instincts took over. All the fear and 'what ifs' disappeared. The wave and the ride were the reasons and nothing else mattered. What an experience. I still get all warm and fuzzy when something evokes total recall of that day like it was happening this afternoon. The stuff we do for waves. What a trip. I never saw Sammy again but I hope he's caught as many waves as I have since then.

That's one story you'll never find on the History Channel. Tom reports that in an odd way, he actually hated to leave when his tour of duty was completed. "For thirteen months, I got to live right on the ocean and surf everyday."

As destiny would have it, his next station was in California. It was another place he didn't want to leave. At that time, both his family and his wife's family were living in Pennsylvania. A mutual decision was made to move back east, but with the stipulation that they had to be close to the ocean. Tom made it back to

Ocean County, living just on the other side of the LBI Causeway, first in Waretown and then in Manahawkin.

Back on the East Coast, Tom had the pleasure of teaching his son Greg all about surfing. Having coached Greg through the grade school sports of baseball and soccer, it was a logical progression to help Tom Ackers coach the Southern Regional High School Surf Team when Greg was part of it. Tom felt that Greg was a talented athlete and could have competed in any number of high school sports. He asked Greg one day, "Why didn't you ever want to go out for sports like football or baseball?" Greg's answer was simple. "Dad, I surf." That simple answer made perfect sense to Tom. It reflected a sentiment that the elder Luker so eloquently summarized:

> *Surfing gives you so much back... physically, spiritually, in terms of camaraderie. In many ways, you don't need anything else.*

Surfing would again greatly influence Tom's life. Pursuing a once in a lifetime dream, Tom teamed up with cinematographer Paul Prewitt from Florida to produce a 16mm film, *Atlantic Crossing*. The goal was to produce footage focusing on the East Coast. From 1988 to 1989, Tom and Paul traveled around the world. They brought along local talent like Justin Citta and Tom's son Greg Luker for footage in Peru, Chili, and Brazil. They were also one of the first to get shots of Kelly Slater in Hawaii. Besides their own footage of surf in North Carolina and Florida, they bought footage of surf in New Hampshire and a solid twenty-foot day at Montauk Point on Long Island, New York.

Once all the filming was completed, they went about promoting the film from New Hampshire to Coral Gables, Florida. Tom remembers the largest number of showings were in Florida - twenty-nine shows in five weeks. The movie was shown in firehouses, Knights of Columbus halls, and if they were lucky, a full-screen, low-rent movie house. A big draw for them was a showing at the Long Beach Island Foundation for the Arts and Sciences in Loveladies. One of the nicest surprises was ESPN buying a minute for one of their commercials. In the end, Tom figures they broke even financially. The experience, however, forever changed his life. While traveling to Puerto Rico for filming, Tom fell in love with the area, and the rest is history.

In 1990, initially apprehensive, Tom purchased a Surf Hostile at Rincon in Puerto Rico. The deciding factor was its view from atop the cliff. There was no way he could turn down the postcard view of the ocean from that vantage point. His job basically included taking reservations, keeping the bathrooms and linen clean, giving advice for food, traveling, surfing, etc., and surfing two to three times a day. "It was my job to surf. If guests arrived and I wasn't there to welcome them, there was never a guilt trip. Instead, my patrons usually greeted me with: 'How was it?'"

The hostile was capable of holding up to thirty guests and was typically filled to capacity between Thanksgiving and Easter. In fact, sometimes it was overfilled. If patrons knew a swell was coming, especially if the conditions had fallen short earlier during the stay, they literally begged to be able to stay longer. Many offered to pay to just sleep on the couch to grab a few extra prime waves.

Tom operated the hostile for ten years and still says, "It was the best job I ever had. Over the years, I had 3,000 best friends who I could surf with anytime I wanted." Tom still lives in Puerto Rico and these days he is a general contractor for various construction projects. Several of his guests, who he met when they were in their late teens, have now returned to Puerto Rico with their families and have asked him to build houses for them.

At fifty-seven, Tom still believes, "If you're surfing, life is good. I'm still surfing!"

Surfing Swami

Swami is the Hindu designation for a religious teacher. There are only a handful of individuals on the East Coast, primarily in the New York City area, who lead Hindu believers in their religion.

Swami Param directs the Classical Yoga Hindu Academy in Manahawkin, New Jersey, which presently meets at the Mill Creek Community Center.

I have to admit, Swami Param didn't exactly fit my preconceived notion of what a swami should be like. Yes, he is extremely articulate, introspective, and soft-spoken. He is able to assume the cross-legged position, and not flinch for a whole interview while I had to change my position fifteen times. On the other hand, this Collingswood, N.J. native is light-haired, fair-skinned, definitely blue-eyed . . . and he surfs. How could it be? In his own words, "First there was Hinduism in a little way, then surfing in a big way, then Hinduism in a very big way."

Param was introduced to surfing by his brother in 1964. Throughout high school they shared a 9'8" Malibu pop-out surfboard. Initially they traveled with the family for weekends on Long Beach Island. If they didn't have access to other accommodations, they also took Fitz up on his offer to sleep on the floor at Rick Surf Shop. The family bought a house in Beach Haven in 1967.

When Param was twenty-one, with all the money he had saved, he spent a year and a half island hopping. Surfboard wrapped snugly in a sleeping bag, and sometimes "hardly eating," Param traveled throughout the Caribbean. He found surf in Puerto Rico, Barbados, St. Thomas, Dominica, Martinique, and Trinidad. He describes one of his best surfing experiences in Tobago where he lived for six months. It was here that he stumbled upon an incredible right point break in the winter that he rode all by himself.

Param's days of traveling were far from over, but amazingly, there would be almost a twenty year stretch when he wouldn't touch a surfboard. As a young teenager, he had heard the word "yoga" and curiously investigated the dictionary definition. An interest was sparked that he continued to casually res©earch until he made the decision to actively pursue Hindu Monastic Studies when he was twenty-four years old.

Param underwent a twelve year "student period" with Hindu Missions located in California, Hawaii, and Sri Lanka (South

India). He then entered the "yogi phase" which involved seclusion and meditation for almost five years. He traveled to Hindu communities in Indonesia, China, Japan, and Trinidad. In the Fiji Islands, where he spent a year and a half, he was asked by the local Hindu community to teach. That is when he received the distinction of "swami."

Param returned to the East Coast and got back on a surfboard in 1996. He has been leading the Manahawkin-based Classical Yoga Hindu Academy since 1997. Swami Param leads all levels of followers in Hatha Yoga (worshipful postures), Bhakiti Yoga (devotions), and Raja Yoga (meditation), to name a few. There is even a "dawn patrol" sunrise meditation service in the summer. It is held, where else, but on the beach on LBI.

Param sees amazing similarities between what happens in a Hindu temple and what happens on the beach. "Before you even walk into the temple, you see rows of shoes outside." Everyone enters the temple with bare feet. This is certainly not unlike the site along our dune fences lined with sandals on a summer day. "People go into the temple to tap into joy and youthfulness. Once inside, you can't tell the doctors from the lawyers from the laymen. When they leave there is a glow about them . . . hopefully more than just sunburn." The surfing experience itself "pumps you up with *shakti*." Shakti is a Sanskrit (language of the Hindu Religion) term for energy. "At times, human nature comes into play—competitiveness and hogging waves. These all short circuit the experience. Ultimately, surfing is a true fluid mystical experience." Param was quick to point out that the roots of surfing go back to kahunas, priests, and Hawaiian royalty who fully realized the natural mystical connection. "Every surfer learns to respect and revere or 'worship' the elements. The surfing lifestyle begins with physical, mental, and emotional preparation— not unlike the classic yogas of Hinduism. It becomes a natural religious ritual with one being opened up to ecstatic inner experiences. The benefit of clean living becomes abundantly clear."

One of Swami's most memorable surfing moments didn't even happen in the water. It happened during the period of Hindu study when he was away from the sport. He reports that the event had a profound impact on his surfing, and his life.

> *Being in love with surfing (any true surfer knows the feeling), the initial separation is extremely painful. While in the Ashram (a Hindu monastery), I experienced a profound meditative vision that helped me put the surfing lifestyle and the Hindu/Yogic lifestyle into a meaningful perspective. Like a movie, in the 'mind's eye,' I saw this perfect tubing wave in front of me. I then realized there was no board! Every surfer seeks that quiet elliptical center of a tubing wave. This elliptical shape is not only in breaking waves but all around us . . . spinning galaxies, the eye of a hurricane, a spiral conch shell, and fundamental DNA. It is also vividly portrayed in the Hindu temple by an elliptical shaped stone called a Shiva Lingam. This ancient object of worship is a constant reminder of one's soulful core.*

For more information about the Classical Yoga Hindu Academy, you can view the website: *classyoga@aol.com* or contact Swami Param at: (609) 607-0846.

Swami Param in tune with the mystical flow of the sea.

Poling Productions

Jack and Clark Poling have compiled surf footage from just about every angle you can imagine. They have used cameras mounted on surfboards and strapped to their backs. Clark has been known to swim his hand-held camera out in surf that is twenty-five feet high. His scariest moment was actually high above the water, when the helicopter ladder he was on came loose and fell fifty feet into the ocean. Clark was unscathed, but the camera was lost.

That wasn't the first camera that the two brothers lost. There was also the family super-eight camera that Jack placed in a not-so-waterproof housing of a plastic bag. It was intended to capture some of the earliest footage of the Polings and their friends surfing Long Beach Island as kids.

The Poling family had a summer home in Haven Beach. Older brother, Barkley, was the first to use a surfboard. Jack was four years old at the time and was determined to steal his brother's surfboard every time it washed into shore. He had to wait until he was six years old to officially purchase his own Hobie Silver

Bullet from Ron Jon Surf Shop. Clark, who is three years younger, was soon in the water right behind them.

The inspiration for filmmaking came from a high school teacher who encouraged Jack to help make a promotional film for the school he was attending. As a hobby, Jack continued to amass footage of surfing exploits wherever he went. This surfing footage gained a reputation at LBI parties and was a frequent request. Recognizing the popularity of his work, Jack edited his best material and put together his first surfing film: *Pressure Drop*. Included in this film was impressive footage of the surf on LBI following Hurricane Belle that arrived on August 9, 1976. The hurricane brought a rare combination of warm water and double-overhead surf to the Northeast. Surfers flocked to the island, just as vacationers returned from a voluntary evacuation of the entire island.

With a bit of luck and persistence, Jack convinced his next door neighbor, who was also president of the Haven Beach Yacht Club, to allow showings of his 8mm surfing movie at the club. In the summer of 1978, *Pressure Drop*, appeared to packed houses for two shows a night, on three separate dates. Back then, the audio was a disc jockey transitioning music from two turn tables.

About this time, Clark also became increasingly interested in surfing cinematography. A competitive high school swimmer, it was natural for Clark to gravitate toward the water shots while Jack worked from the beach. Clark has since developed several underwater housing including the "bubble cam" that provides an aquarium-look to images. The ability to film both from the land and the water gave the brothers a wide range of creative options when editing their material.

In 1980, Jack and Clark packed all their movie equipment and jumped on a plane to Hawaii. They didn't know anybody there. In fact, they didn't even have any lodging arrangements. By the time they made it to their presumed destination of the North Shore, it was already dark. In a twist of fate, as they struggled, walking with all their equipment down the street, they caught the eye of big wave rider and surfing legend, Mark Foo (1958-1994). He offered them a rented room in a hostile that he ran. That relationship would become one of the "ins" they needed professionally, but also one of the relationships they always treasured personally.

Through Mark Foo, the Polings were introduced to many of the 'surfing greats.' Jack remembers showing footage of the 1978 Seaside Pro Surfing Event to professional surfers, Shaun Thomson and Rabbit Bartholomew in someone's living room in Hawaii. Mark even traveled to LBI, bringing professional surfers, Mike Parsons and Hans Hederman with him. Mrs. Poling graciously baked them all chocolate chip cookies while Clark and Jack went about business, filming these big wave riders ripping up Harvey Cedars. The 1989 video cassette recording, *LBI Saltwater High*, has wonderful footage from that trip, including Hawaiian reaction to Jersey jellyfish.

The Polings bought a car while they were in Hawaii for $75. Mark helped Clark re-paint the car, including the inscription "Surf Attack" on the roof. *Surf Attack* became the title of their next surf movie released in 1981. The movie turned out to be a lot more popular than the car. The Polings left the car in Hawaii with Mark when they returned to the East Coast. Not long after, it was blown-up by some Aussie surfers.

Mark graciously used his notoriety as a *98 Rock* disc jockey in Honolulu to promote Jack and Clark's 1983 movie, *Wet Lips*. Mark helped set up interviews and endorsed their projects in whatever way he could. It obviously paid-off. They filled Kaiser High School with 4,000 people for one showing.

In 1985, Poling Productions' *Summer Surfari*, premiered at the Long Beach Island Foundation of the Arts & Sciences but surfers weren't the only ones hooting about their work. The *Solid Gold* television program was impressed enough to purchase a five-minute segment. Bill Delaney who produced the *Free Ride* movies also used some of the Poling footage. Poling Productions also shared some of their footage with other film makers like the Contin Brothers in Hawaii and Steve Spalding in California.

Besides Hawaii, Jack and Clark have filmed all up and down the East Coast, California, Mexico, Australia, Barbados, French Indonesia, and the Caribbean. Clark has survived more than his share of closeouts at Pipeline, with camera in hand. They've met interesting people from all over the world including a Rastafarian tribe in Barbados who devotes their whole life to surfing.

Poling Productions went on to produce the following works on video cassette:

Surf Attack II (1987), *LBI Saltwater High* (1988), *Surfing Florida, Local Style* (1991), and *Atomic Freestyle Jetskiing* (1992). These titles are currently being remastered for DVD release. Compilation DVD's entitled *Storm Surf, Caribunga,* and *Exotic Waves* are in the works as is *LBI Saltwater High II* which will be released Summer 2003. Also look for the surfing documentary on DVD: *Kelly Slater—Born to Surf.* Anyone interested in information about any of these releases can contact Poling Productions at: P.O. Box 620626, Oviedo, FL 32762 or www.PolingProductions.com.

The Polings are also working on a project that is a new "East Coast news and reviews surfing DVD magazine," that will premiere summer of 2003. More information about that can be found at www.x-waves.com.

When Jack and Clark aren't filming water sports, they work in the professional realm of legal multimedia services. They do everything from restoring and enhancing images to preparing presentations for jury review.

Jack and Clark have never been able to get too far away from filming storms and the waves they produce. Jack still remembers Hurricane Belle that he considers the "catalyst" for his first movie. In that storm's fury, "the downstairs sliding door blew in just before we watched a ten foot wave roll down the street in Haven Beach." The brothers have footage of Hurricane Iwa on the North Shore of Oahu, Hurricane Andrew in South Florida, and the "Palm Beach Tidal Wave" for which Jack has "appeared on every talk show known to man except Oprah."

While Jack and Clark are presently living in Florida, there's no denying their LBI connection. The surfing tradition has already been passed on to the next generation with Jack's children: Kelsey(11), Spencer(10), Colby(7), and Clark's children: Chelsea(16) and Max(12) all being avid surfers. According to Jack, "I think someday we will end up coming back to LBI. I would like our kids can experience the same 'Saltwater High' that we did as kids."

(A) Hans Hederman on surfari in Harvey Cedars (B) Mark Foo and Mike Parsons experience "Joisy jellies" in Cedars. (C) The "Surf Attack" mobile hand-painted by Mark and Clark. (D) Unknown Surfer powering through the remnants of Hurricane Belle (1976). All images were obtained from the 1988 release of *LBI Saltwater High* by Poling Productions and Back to the Shore Video Magazine.

Rocket Power

Twister. Squid. Reggie. Otto Rocket. Do the names sound a little bit like WWF competitors? Guess again. They are the stars of Nickelodeon's *Rocket Power* cartoon which first aired August 16, 1999. Former Long Beach Island lifeguard Michael Bloom was responsible for the early success of the show which you can still catch on the Nick channel.

The idea started with Klasky Csupo, the creator of another cartoon hit, the *Rugrats*. Klasky needed to find people who understood the beach culture and what it meant to be a kid growing up at the beach. Two New Jerseyites fit the bill: Andy McElfresh from the Avalon/Stone Harbor area, and LBI's own Michael Bloom. Andy and Michael worked together during the early stages of development of the project. Michael would go on to write and produce the first two seasons of approximately forty episodes.

Rocket Power is geared to the six to twelve year-old crowd but definitely has wide appeal. All beachgoers can live vicariously through these characters who spend their days surfing, skating, and snowboarding. There is a universal story line about fun but also responsibility. According to Michael, "It focuses on the time in life when the umbilical cord is cut. All of a sudden, mom and dad aren't around every minute of everyday and the characters are in situations that they have to learn their *own* lessons. The writing staff takes a lot of care to emphasize the importance of personal responsibility in everything from relationships to water safety. You may pick up a few shore nuances like the term "shoobie" or the character "Tice" who oversees the "lifeguard in training program." Don't be misled, however. In real life, Tice of the Long Beach Township Beach Patrol (LBTBP) is more mellow than ex-Marine Tice on the big screen.

Michael has been living in Santa Monica, California since 1996 where he surfs all year. Rewind back to childhood . . . Michael was a New Jersey native from Morristown. He spent every summer of his life, through his early twenties, at his grandparent's home in Spray Beach. His real introduction to surfing came through the LBTBP where he worked from 1984 to 1986 and again in 1990. He fine-tuned his surfing skills "training" on the rescue paddleboards while working on the beach.

Early on, Michael planned business trips to the West Coast so he could "hang out and crash" with fellow LBTBP lifeguard, Chris Koerner. Since then, Michael has been one of the people opening his door to fellow guards. There is a standing joke that they should have a LBI Chapter of the famous San Onofre Surf Club.

Michael has noticed that his greatest professional successes have involved beach and surf-related programming. He was working in marketing and advertising in 1990 when he had the opportunity to work on the concept of the *MTV Beach House*. He was the writer and television producer for the program's first four seasons. This included two summers in the Hamptons and two summers in Malibu. Michael is especially proud of using his influence to broadcast Surfrider Foundation public service announcements to a national audience during those "early beach house days." The short spots helped educate people about pollution, responsible beach use, and also helped the member base grow exponentially. Michael has been on the National Advisory Board for the Surfrider Foundation since that time.

His other work includes producing a surf video for Billabong Surf Academy: *Surfing A to Z*. This video received great reviews in *Surfer* and *Surfing* magazines and also won an award at the Surfer Magazine Poll Awards.

Michael is presently trying to develop a family drama/comedy called *Summer Land* which is based on beach experiences that he and his sister had growing up, where else, but on LBI.

There's no doubt that Michael's LBI roots are strong. "That's where I fell in love with the ocean and now I take it with me to other places." That has included the living rooms of a national audience, of all ages, for over a decade. And as for surfing . . ."Surfing is about escape, challenge, and fun. I've made the best friends in the world through surfing. I couldn't imagine life without it."

Rocket Power's writer and producer, Michael Bloom (left) catches up with the real life "Tice" in California.

Jason Murray

Who hasn't taken a surfing photo and secretly hoped to see their name in print under it? Let's face it, only a handful of folks ever get that distinction. Even a fewer number of people derive a regular pay check from a surfing magazine. What about being a photo editor? That's reserved for someone who has been around surfing for thirty or more years and who is from California or Hawaii, right?

Not so for the twenty-eight year old, Jason Murray. He's been fulfilling his dream of being able to surf and travel, and even make a living out of it. He is THE Photo Editor for *Surfer*, a magazine read monthly by over 500,000 people worldwide. Jason is proof that "no one should ever feel confined because of where they are from." Born in Mount Holly and raised in Crosswicks, N.J. he spent every summer in Beach Haven from three weeks old until the age of eighteen. He remembers standing on a styrofoam board on a sandbar as a toddler and later riding the infamous 'Pocket Rockets.' He caught a wave on his first fiberglass surfboard when he was seven years old and has been at it ever since. Once he could get a ride or drive himself, he was hitting the surf year-round.

Jason, a.k.a. "Gremmy," fondly remembers competing in some of the local shop contests through Body Language and Freedom Surf Shops, as well as a few ESA events. Surfing Holyoke, Leeward-Nelson, and Wooden Jetty were his mainstays with his contemporaries: Sammy Zuegner, Chuck Labin, The McGlynn brothers, John Lampman, and Mike Roth. He looked up to the older guys like: Eric Kertesz (Jughead), Creighton M., Kurt Horenski, Dave Voris, Billy Lutz, Ron Cox, Dean Harkness, Greg Luker, and Justin Citta.

When Jason wasn't surfing, he was entrenched in skateboarding. In fact, his first photos, taken when he was ten years old, were of his skateboarding buddies, Sam Zuegner and Brian Lampman, pulling moves at places like the Beach Haven Elementary School, local bank, post office, and backyard mini ramps.

Jason moved from New Jersey in 1992 to pursue a degree in business economics. His criteria for choosing a college was pretty clear cut. The school had to have a good academic reputation and afford the opportunity for good surf. Jason found that the University of California—Santa Cruz, fit the bill perfectly. While there, he jumped on the opportunity to do a three-month internship in the photo department of *Surfer* magazine in the summer of 1995, under the guidance of Jeff Divine and Tom Servais. This would be a life-changing experience as he realized that you could make a living, albeit a simple one, from being a surf photographer. While later attending graduate school for a degree in applied economics & finance, Jason accepted a position as a contributing photographer to the magazine he had read as a grom.

In a seemingly fairy-tale story, Jason was offered a position as the assistant photo editor in 1997. Realizing that a career in finance and banking was not his true calling, he happily accepted and came on board that summer. A year and a half later, he was promoted to photo editor, a position he has maintained ever since. Of the experience, Jason offers that he is extremely grateful for the opportunity and for all the people that he has met along the way. There is no denying that his "love and passion for the ocean" was kindled during his earliest experiences at the Jersey shore. He's proud to be something of a flag bearer now, raising awareness and respect for the East Coast surfer, and the waves they surf, no matter what the conditions. He takes pride in helping *Surfer* magazine provide the proper East Coast coverage. He's using the opportunity to give the coastline that taught him so much, something in return.

Jason is especially sympathetic to the photographers from the northeast "who are dedicated to their craft in the middle of the winter, not just the warm tropical season." If you think that you might have some talent, Jason recommends that you keep sending in your best images to his attention. He is always looking for new talent and is especially excited when he can help "one of his own kind."

Jason is quick to point out some other success stories in the world of surf photography. Of John Bilderback, who summered for years in Barnegat Light, Jason says, "He is perhaps one of the best long lens photographers in the world. He has been at the top of his game for over twenty years, most of which have been spent on the North Shore of Oahu." Jason is also stoked about LBI local, Chris Pfeil, whose work is just coming on the scene, and recently appeared in an article for *The Surfers Journal.* Jason looks forward to seeing a lot more of Chris' work.

As for future plans, Jason says, "Right now I just really enjoy being editor of the best surf magazine in the world. It's a badge that I wear with honor. I look forward to the day when the world champ will call New Jersey home."

Bilderback's Lens

John Bilderback is one of the most-talented surf photographers in the world today. He has been a senior photographer at *Surfer* magazine for over ten years. His pictures have appeared in every major surfing and windsurfing magazine as well as some mainstream magazines like: *MAX, Rolling Stone* and *FHM.*

John studied photography at the University of California-San Diego and then did an apprenticeship with Aaron Chang. Aaron introduced him to Sunset Beach in Hawaii where he has been ever since. That's where John photographs some of the largest waves in the world. "When the waves get really huge, I take shots from a jet ski that I drive for myself."

John's first apprenticeship, however, really began on Long Beach Island. He fondly remembers his older brother Pete taking him bodysurfing in the sandbar shore break of Barnegat Light where he grew up. "I remember ducking under the waves and clinging to the sandy bottom, trying not to get peeled back 'over the falls.' I've been doing that for a career ever since."

John started surfing in 1972. He and Tim Stempel learned on the longboards they dragged through the seemingly endless

Barnegat Light dunes. "Before long, some older surfers gave us short boards and we were hooked. We rode whatever came along, read *Surfer* magazine and chased tourist girls all summer. Tim always got the girls - he was my hero." The big road trip back then was to Harvey Cedars to surf "Coffee Shop" or Hudson Avenue.

Both Peter and John went on to make a life for themselves, close to the sea. Peter is a sport fisherman, commercial fisherman and tug boat captain. John's move to California for college opened the door to work at *Surfing* magazine in 1982. Even though John has photographed the best surfing conditions in the world, he looks forward to photographing LBI. "When I make annual trips back to see family, I try to get some proof of the good surf I remember at home." John's 2001 trip to the East Coast finally gave him the chance he was looking for. That's when he documented an epic day on LBI that made the world jealous.

John had driven all night from Cape Hatteras where he had been shooting for *Surfer*. He arrived in Surf City around dawn. He headed down to Holyoke Avenue in Beach Haven where he captured several incredible shots that were featured in the article, "Heat Wave: Sweating out hurricane season along the East Coast." Included in this was a shot of Sammy Zuegner. That one picture got a two-page photo spread and also a headline on the cover of *Surfer* as "The Best East Coast Tube Ever Seen." That's the kind of recognition that a photographer works for his entire life. All up and down the East Coast that day, surfers were enjoying some of the best surf in recent memory. Unfortunately, the accomplishments and joy of that day were sadly overshadowed by the national tragedy that was unfolding on September 11, 2001. John remembers seeing smoke in the distance from New York City and everyone feeling that they were in a daze.

In the world of surf photography, John is one of the most sought after individuals in the business. His client list includes almost all the major surf manufacturers. He has also worked for companies like Titan Rocket Systems, Disney, and 20th Century

Fox. John sees his future as including more focus on photographing the emerging sport of kitesurfing and also delving into film-making. Despite all John's accomplishments, he has never forgotten his roots:

> The East Coast is lucky to have Long Beach Island and its waves. My friends and I never wished we lived anywhere else. That being said, the list of LBI surfers on the North Shore is pretty long. There are several hardened big wave guys here with humble beginnings like myself. I think we got a taste of good surf and wanted more . . . Our lives being fundamentally shaped by that eighteen mile strip of sand and surf.

Chris Pfeil

"Even before I knew how to surf, I remember looking down the beach and intently watching the surfers in the water. They would always catch my eye." That eye for surfing has paid off, and gained thirty-three-year-old Chris Pfeil recognition as a talented photographer in the surfing community. His work was recently featured in *The Surfer's Journal*, a magazine read by surfers all over the world. The ten page, thirteen picture presentation features Long Beach Island's winter waves and the local surfers who brave them.

Chris was fortunate to be able to spend every summer of his life at his grandparent's home in Loveladies. Early on, he spent a lot of time bodyboarding. When he became a lifeguard, he quickly learned to handle himself on a paddleboard. Interestingly, he didn't start surfing until he was eighteen years old. Chris has more than made up for lost time, living and surfing on LBI year-round since 1994 and traveling for surf whenever he gets the chance.

The surf trip that still stands out the most was his first one. Shortly after college, with camera in hand, Chris and two friends traveled for six months from LBI to Mexico and then throughout Central America, down to Panama. This group gave new meaning to "winging it." They never knew how long they would stay in any place or even what the next night's accommodations would be like. Despite their limited Spanish, they surfed the coast and also made their way inland to some of the major cities to get a feel for the cultural centers. Chris describes it as the best learning experience of his life, meeting new people and learning about different cultures. He was able to capture much of the culture on film with his newly acquired photography skills.

Chris' talent for photography wasn't always apparent to him. He took his first photography course while struggling to get through Stockton State College. It boosted his GPA and has since opened up several opportunities. Although Chris never really intended to pursue commercial photography, his talented work has been paying some bills. Chris was able to team up with another surfing photographer, Jack Ryan, from the Monmouth County area. The result was the first-ever exclusive New Jersey surfing calendar—"Surfing The Garden State: 2003 wave log / tide chart calendar." Public demand for this calendar has exceeded their original expectations. Look for more projects like this from Jack and Chris.

Chris readily admits that he is a jack-of-all-trades. Like many of the locals, he has worked in restaurants and construction. Recently, he has been doing a lot of commercial fishing, which satisfies some of his passion for the water. But, for Chris, there's nothing quite like being *in* the water and surfing. When Chris gets to combine his love of surfing with his photography skills, the result is magical. Chris has shots taken from second floor decks as well right from the water using his waterproof housing. His pictures aren't the typical, vibrant color close-ups of surfers slashing the wave faces. The shots are black and white and taken from a distance to include the whole environment—surfer, ocean, and beach. His pictures tell it all, and what they're telling the rest of the world is just how good the local surfers and the local waves can be.

You'll find several of Chris' striking photos throughout this book. With so many exceptional shots in his portfolio, it was torture to limit the selection to just a handful. For Chris, his photography is a way to capture some of the natural scenes that we often take for granted. His photo collection tells a whole story of LBI . . . from beachscapes and birds, to commercial fishing and views of the Atlantic City skyline. I personally found some incredible shots of waves that I couldn't stop looking at. Rather than further delay his afternoon surf session, I commissioned him on the spot to mat and frame the set with one of his handsome, handmade wooden frames.

If it's any testimony to Chris' work, I could have looked at his photos for hours. As a surfer himself, he has excellent timing for capturing the surfer and the wave. You also get a deep sense from viewing his work just how much he loves and appreciates the natural beauty of this island.

For more information on *Surfing The Garden State* calendar or viewing shots from Chris' portfolio, contact Chris Pfeil at: (609) 361-3448 or p_feil@hotmail.com.

Reference:

Pfeil, Christopher. "The Quiet Season: Winter Solitude in New Jersey." *The Surfers Journal* 11(4), 2002, 72-81.

Return of the Wooden Surfboard

Wooden surfboards are no longer just a thing of the past. The twenty-eight year old Ben Rasmussen has been doing his homework and created boards that are not only some of the most handsome you'll ever see, they also afford great performance in the surf. Ben built his first wooden board in August 2000 and has worked on fourteen boards since then. The boards have been a learning process in surfboard design as well as woodworking. His quiver now includes a classic 9'6" single fin design (1960s); a 7'8" single fin gun (1970s); a 6'3" twin fin fish (1980s); and modern thrusters of various sizes including a 9'8" longboard that weighs an amazing seventeen pounds.

These works of art are made of combinations of plywood, pine, and cedar. Ben also uses walnut for his tail blocks and accents. The natural patterns of the wood are revitalized with clear epoxy resin. The bottom half of the board that Ben is working on now is actually eighty year old mahogany that a friend salvaged from wall paneling in a demolished home. Ben is especially excited about how the tight grains of this mature wood will look once hit with their glossy finish.

Okay, so it looks good. Does it work? Ben, who has been surfing since he was fourteen years old, rides his wooden boards exclusively. He is so confident in his product that when he travels now, he takes only a wooden board with him and leaves the foam behind. Ben's wooden boards have been surfed up and down the East Coast, California, Mexico, and Panama. When folks first see them the reaction is always the same, "Wow!"

The wooden boards perform slightly different from a foam board. The intricate grid structure inside minimizes the flex that you feel compared to foam. While Ben has successfully been getting his boards lighter and lighter, his shortboards are still slightly heavier than their foam counterparts. Ben finds that this actually provides a performance advantage with greater entry speed into the wave. Compared to foam, Ben would rather be on his wooden board to make it down the face against an offshore wind or just trying to beat out a section. Because of the inherent momemtum in these wooden boards, you can also get away with a smaller board on a small day. Although you would expect a shorter and heavier board to sink in the water, this isn't the case with wood. All the wooden boards offer amazing flotation with their thicker rails and trapped air inside.

Two individuals who inspired Ben were Bob Boyle and his father, Paul Rasmussen. When Ben first started surfing near his family's summer home in Loveladies, he often surfed with Bob Boyle. Boyle was shaping Java Surfboards out of a garage in Loveladies and graciously let Ben watch him. Ben was always intrigued by the process, but didn't think anymore about it until his father finally talked him into trying some woodworking projects after college. With a "precise eye and engineering background," Ben's father has been making beautiful furniture as a hobby for years. Ben's first project was some Adirondack chairs. With that, Ben realized that he not only enjoyed woodworking, but was better at it than he thought. That's when the wheels started turning . . . Ben thought it would be more fulfilling to make a product he could surf, not just sit on.

The task has not been easy. Ben estimates his first board took him over one hundred hours to assemble from start to finish. He can now do one in about thirty hours. His initial Internet search led him to a gentleman in Maui who is making balsa boards. The man sent him some "rough" descriptions. Leaving a lot to be desired, Ben has relied heavily on information from his father "knowing how wood works," board design information, and some trial and error.

Ben describes how the construction of wooden and foam boards contrast. "When you work with a foam board, you're constantly shaving the foam down to get the shape you want. With wood, you are constantly adding pieces and building it up." Five stringers-each three sixteenths of an inch- are the core of the board, carefully shaped to provide the desired rocker. Ben's skills have evolved to the point that he is even able to build concavities into the board. Two planks that are each three sixteenths of an inch are cut using one template. These bottom planks, either solid pieces or multiple glued pieces, are then glued to the stringers. A one by twelve inch piece of wood provides the curved configuration that will become the rail of the surfboard. At this point, the observer starts to really see the design that Ben has been envisioning all along.

There are still hours of work ahead. Depending on the length of the board, as many as sixty to seventy cross pieces are arranged between the stringers to provide additional stability. These pieces may be as close as three inches apart in high stress areas. All of the boards must be installed with vent plugs. Since there is trapped air inside the board, it is necessary to release built-up pressure, especially as the air expands with increased heat. All wooden pieces inside the board are carefully given a thin layer of epoxy in order to "waterproof the inside" for longevity. Ben has been successful mounting the fins by either glassing them in, using fin boxes, or the FCS system.

Once the top planks are glued in position, there is still more sanding and shaping to be done. With a craftsman's precision, Ben softens all the curves and brings out the brilliance of the wood. The final component is the glassing phase. Less fiberglass cloth needs to be used since wood is inherently stronger than foam. While more expensive, Ben prefers to use epoxy instead of resin since it affords greater strength, lightness, and is less toxic to use.

Ben works on his boards in his Surf City home as well as at his father's wood shop in Loveladies. When sawdust isn't flying in Ben's house, it serves as his office. Ben is a residential real estate appraiser by profession. Working from home lets him surf when needed. "Surfing drives everything I do. I knew I'd never make it as a pro surfer or make a living out of it, but this is something I can do that I really enjoy."

Ben isn't set up to mass produce the boards, but is willing to make custom boards if someone is interested. The material costs alone for the boards are over $300. Comparatively speaking, there is no denying that the board is more expensive and more time-consuming to make. But, if you're looking for the feel of a slightly different board, Ben has gone to great lengths to insure that his boards ride as good as they look. Ben's main focus with every board is function in the water. A secondary consideration is that you're guaranteed to attract attention carrying this piece of artwork under your arm. When your significant other asks if you really need another board, you can always say that you've never ridden one like this before.

Inquiries are welcome by contacting Ben Rasmussen at: (609) 618-8501 or BKWAVE@aol.com.

(**Left**) Ben Rasmussen holds the "guts" of a wooden surfboard. Note the five stringers positioned vertically. As many as sixty crosspieces will then be placed perpendicular to these. (**Right**) Ben's unique wooden quiver

Joe's Smile

Joe DeGennaro grew up in Surf City. He and younger brother, Matt, were veritable water people, bodyboarding and surfing every chance that they got. Early on, Joe excelled in bodyboarding competition. Through high school, Joe competed on the Southern Regional High School Surf Team (class of 1987). He also competed in Eastern Surfing Association (ESA) contests, placing as high as second place in the East Coast Region in bodyboard competition.

Always an avid skateboarder, it wasn't until Joe move to California in 1993 that he became involved in competitive downhill skateboarding. While our flat Long Beach Island never lent itself to this extreme sport, Pacific Beach did. Joe is a member of Dregs—an international downhill skateboarding team based in Pacific Beach, California. This group, equipped with custom-fit aerodynamic helmets and leather bodysuits, are able to achieve speeds approaching sixty miles per hour on a skateboard. Joe is considered to be one of the sport's pioneers. He represented the sport in downhill skateboarding competition when it was an exhibition sport during the X-Games in San Diego.

Joe is gifted not only athletically but artistically as well. He got his start on LBI, when he worked for DK Designs. Once in California, Joe worked as a graphic artist for a San Diego company. Following his artistic passion, Joe has painted numerous works of art as well. His unique style and use of vivid acrylic colors on large (four foot by eight foot) canvas even earned him a showing in a prestigious San Diego gallery.

With no seeming end to Joe's talents, he is also the inventive mind behind Terra-Wax. It is the first and only surfing wax product that is completely environmentally-friendly. The idea and the name for this product came to Joe in a dream. He then combined extensive library research and hundreds of trial batches in crock pots in his personal kitchen. The end result was several ruined crock pots **and** a nontoxic and biodegradable product composed of greater than fifty percent natural minerals. Joe didn't stop there, however. He also insisted on packaging the wax using paper that is made from treeless-plant based papers. Even the wax combs were made from recycled plastics that were developed to break down without releasing toxins.

Joe introduced the new wax product to California surf shops in 1995. The orders started pouring in while Joe was still working out of his kitchen. In order to keep up with demand, Joe sought assistance from investors and distributors who have been managing the details of this unique product ever since. It has appeared on surf shop shelves as far away as Japan and Australia with sales approaching a million bars of wax.

Unfortunately, tragedy struck in May of 2002. Joe was involved in a skateboarding accident in California and suffered multiple injuries. Some doctors gave him little hope of survival. Today he is recovering at a rehabilitation center in New Jersey.

Joe's mother, Michelle, fondly recalls the impact surfing has had on his life. She looks forward to the day when he can get his toes in the sand again. She remembers how Joe spoke of how surfing was something that he would do forever. "It meant a lot to him, sitting out there on the water and being connected to the universe. It was always beautiful and powerful for him."

Joe has always lived a life devoted to preserving the earth's natural resources. He is one of the rare folks who actually "practices what he preaches." As a vegan, Joe doesn't eat any meat or animal byproducts. His primary mode of transportation around town has always been a skateboard. Joe is quoted as having said, "I'll keep it green 'til the day I die and hope that by being a good example, others will do the same."

All of us in the LBI Surfing Family send our best wishes to Joe and his family during this period of recovery. We are all proud of Joe's many accomplishments and admire his strong environmental commitments. Everyone I interviewed was quick to remark about Joe's "big heart" and how his presence, with his incredible smile, immediately lit up any room. We can't wait to see Joe's big smile again.

Joe on a surfing trip in Mexico in 1992. Also pictured is his unique surfing product - *Terra Wax* and one of his striking pieces of artwork - *Blue Girl*.

Southern Regional High School Surfing Team

The Southern Regional High School Surf Team was formed in 1985 thanks to the persistent efforts of **Noel Huelsenbeck (SRHS class of 1986)**. Growing up in Ship Bottom, Noel was already involved in the surfing scene—surfing Eastern Surfing Association (ESA) contests and providing ding repair for Skip Miller at Line Drive surfboards. While working at Line Drive, he would occasionally hear conversations about competitors in the National Scholastic Surfing Association (NSSA), a nationwide high school surfing organization.

Noel started to ask questions about how they could make it happen at SRHS. One of the stipulations was that the coach had to be someone on the high school faculty. Noel's father, William Huelsenbeck, suggested **Tom Ackers (SRHS class of 1964)** an industrial arts teacher at the high school. The elder Huelsenbeck is a lifelong resident of Ship Bottom and also its mayor since 1999. He was an avid surfer in his youth and had grown up surfing with Tom Ackers. He knew that the team would be in competent hands under Tom's leadership.

Noel recalls Tom getting things in place at an administrative level for final approval by the Board of Education. Ultimately, the Board agreed that the SRHS Surfing Team would have a positive impact by keeping students in the water instead of on the streets after school. Team members would be required to meet the same academic requirements as their peers in other intramural sports. They would also have to pass a swim test. Since the team's inception, the Long Beach Township Beach Patrol has been providing their support by testing the surfers on water safety and providing their presence during NSSA-sanctioned surfing meets held in Long Beach Township.

Team members are responsible for their own equipment—surfboards and wetsuits. In the "old days," students would pile up their boards in a corner in Mr. Acker's classroom. As the number of participants increased, an outside shed was procured to safely store all the equipment. SRHS has always provided bus transportation to and from the surf meets during the official team season. From September through November, there are approximately eight meets with other teams in the league. In recent years, students also have the option to use bus transportation for the three weekly practices.

The spring is considered "open" NSSA season. High school surfers have the opportunity to surf independently in NSSA sanctioned events. The goal of these events is to gain a spot on the NSSA national team which is the equivalent of an All-American Team for traditional sports.

Surfing will never be a "traditional sport" in New Jersey because of its limited scope. Even coastal schools can not always get enough participants. Consequently, the league membership is always changing. It is now the largest it has been in years, with a total of twelve schools. Like any sport, Acker points out that there is the opportunity for character development as well as fun. Far from detracting from education, members of the surf team knew that they had to make it to class and make the grade in order to practice and compete. Ackers made sure of that. One of the pay-offs has been that NSSA members could apply for college scholarships offered solely to surfers.

In 1984, when SRHS first joined the league, the categories consisted of men, women, and bodyboarders. Today, the bodyboarding category has been replaced with a longboarding category. Over the years, SRHS has had as many as thirty surfers on the team. When it comes time for the meets, however, the number of competitors is limited to: twelve entries in the men's (shortboard) category; three in the women's category; and three longboarders.

In the 1980s other high school teams in the league were: Mainland, Holy Spirit, Atlantic City, Wildwood, and Lower Cape May. Noel remembers when one of their fiercest competitors was Dean Randazzo from Holy Spirit High School. Dean became one of the finest surfing competitors ever from the state of New Jersey. At one time, Dean was ranked in the top forty-four in the world!

Noel's legacy is the success of the SRHS team members, some of whom have made their mark on the national surfing scene. After high school graduation, Noel joined the Navy and was stationed in San Diego. His work schedule from 3 P.M. to 10 P.M. allowed him plenty of time to surf everyday. After the service, Noel remained in California to enjoy the warmer climate and more consistent surf. He made his mark on the business world exhibiting the same tenacity he used when he started the surfing team. He owned and operated several companies over the years, and currently owns a telecommunications consulting company in Del Mar.

Noel works at his home, which lets him be available for his eleven-year-old daughter, and yes, to surf, when the need arises. Noel says that if it's 3'-4' and glassy, he may step away from the desk. If it's 10' plus, even his best customers have to wait. We hate to let the "cat out of the bag," but if you call him and the message says, "Sorry, I either stepped away from my desk, or I'm on the other line . . ." the other line just may be a surfboard leash.

Tom Ackers capably kept the SRHS Surf Team afloat from 1984 to 1998. That's when he passed the reigns to Will Zylinski. After fifteen years, Tom, who is the father of six, ages fourteen through twenty-four, decided it was time to spend his after-school hours watching his children compete in sports.

Tom still surfs when he can. It has always been a part of his life. Even Tom's father surfed briefly when he was stationed in Hawaii, just after Pearl Harbor. Tom bought his first board from Ron DiMenna's attic in 1962. Before the days of bars of wax, he remembers covering the board with paraffin that was intended for canning. He surfed briefly for the Ron Jon Surf Team but through high school was committed competitively to wrestling. Later, as SRHS faculty, Tom coached wrestling to several surfer-wrestlers like Chuck Barfoot, Steve Jones and son Gary Jones.

* * *

One of Tom Acker's stars early on was **Justin Citta (SRHS class of 1989)**. Justin started surfing in 1984 when he was fourteen years old. Two years later, he was competing for the SRHS Team and was also making an impact at ESA events. Justin's best competition year was 1988 when he competed in the ESA Junior Men's category, placing first at the Northeast Regionals, fourth at the East Coast Championships, and tenth at the National Amateur Championships.

Justin has always felt that he does his best surfing outside of the competition arena. However, it did give him an opportunity to watch and learn from other top surfers like Kelly Slater from Cocoa Beach, Florida. Since Kelly is just two years younger, they competed in the same division at several East Coast events. Justin held his own against Kelly who went on to professional surfing world champion status, an unprecedented consecutive six times. (More proof that you can't take East Coast surfers too lightly).

Stoked on the surfing experience, Justin spent about six months in Hawaii after graduating high school. He earned sponsorship from companies like Dragon (eyewear), O'Neil (wetsuits), Reef (footwear), and a ten-year stint with Rusty (surfboards). He has traveled around the world to places like Mexico, Barbados, South Africa, and Brazil where he met his wife Carolina.

These days, Justin is a carpenter in Ocean County which gives him the freedom to get out in the water when the surf is up. He still surfs about three contests per year and has sponsorship from Smith (eyewear), Globe (apparel), and JC Surfboards of Hawaii.

* * *

I was able to catch up with **Sammy Zuegner (SRHS class of 1993)**, who, after spending some time in Hawaii and Florida, is now in San Clemente, California. He's one of the rare folks who has actually made a living in the surfing industry, and he's been at it for ten years now. As a "photo pro," he teams up with some high-profile photographers and spends a day in the water, "posing" the best way he knows how—full speed on a closing tube. Sammy's tools of the trade include a weather map and a telephone to make arrangements by car or by plane to the next full-on photo session.

Sammy has surfed throughout North, South, and Central Americas. This September, Sammy and friends are planning a trip to Alaska. He's been fortunate to have plenty of sponsorship, from companies like: Lost Enterprises (apparel), Spyder (surfboards), Nixon (watches), DaKine (surfing accessories), XCel (wetsuits).

According to Sammy, "Even though I've surfed all over, surfing on LBI has always been a gem for me." Sammy has appeared in print several times on LBI waves. Who can forget the two-page photo spread of Sammy in *Surfer* Winter 2001? You may remember the teaser on the cover, "The Best East Coast Tube Ever Seen," with none other than Sammy, peaking out of the green room from Holyoke Avenue. Sammy's picture has appeared a half dozen times in *Surfer* and *Surfing* magazines. You can find him most recently in the February 2003 edition of *Surfer*, ready to head out into Hurricane Isidore in Corpus Christi, Texas. Additionally, he has appeared in *Men's Journal* and *TransWorld*.

Sammy has also been working his way up the corporate ladder and is the national sales manager for Spyder Surfboards. When he's not at the office, he's at the beach, serving as a team manager for the Spyder Surf Team which includes some very promising talent. One of Sammy's biggest stokes is personally training a nine-year-old and a twelve-year-old who right now are top in the nation for their age divisions.

Sammy's future plans? "Making it last as long as I can. Usually when you surf, you have to have a lot of 'odd jobs' to make a living and still get out in the water. I couldn't imagine life without surfing. Fortunately, I've been lucky that I found a way to make a living out of it."

* * *

Ben McBrien (SRHS class of 1995) is from Manahawkin and still lives and works in the area. As a carpenter, he arranges his schedule to get out in the water whenever he can. He's had sponsorship since he was in high school, with backing from companies like Rip Curl (wetsuits), WRV (surfboards), Smith (eyewear), and DaKine (surfing accessories). He's placed as high as third in the ESA East Coast Championships (1997), and also competed in world qualifying series (WQS) contests for the Association of Surfing Professionals (ASP). Ben's "crowning moment" was this past fall in the first-ever Garden State Grudge Match, where he made the semi-finals. Ben first got his feet wet when he was eight years old and rode one of his father's old surfboards. The passion has never dwindled and Ben still enjoys "living the dream."

* * *

Randy Townsend (SRHS class of 1998) of Surf City, has a list of surfing accomplishments almost as long as his arms. Genetically-gifted with a long reach, and what some people suspect are webs between his fingers, Randy is also an unbeatable opponent in local paddleboard races. Add to that, Randy's endless hours in the water. He's been surfing since he was eleven, and hitting it hard, year-round, since the time he was thirteen. Randy trains in and out of the water to not only improve his skill but also his stamina. All the hard work has definitely been paying off. Randy has sponsors like McCrystal (surfboards), DaKine (surfing accessories), Globe (apparel), and Cobian Soul Wear (apparel). His achievements are starting to stack-up:

> Member of 2000 U.S. Surfing Team
> 2000 East Coast Champion
> 2000 NSSA Nationals - Fifth Place
> Three-time Northeast Regionals Men's Champion
> Two-time Open Regionals
> Two Pro/Am Wins
> First NJ surfer ever to win a WQS-sanctioned event

* * *

"It would be hard to imagine life if I couldn't surf." For **Jamie Dewitt (SRHS class of 2001)** surfing has been a part of her life, her entire life. Growing up in North Beach Haven, where she still makes her home, she was bodyboarding in the ocean when she was two years old. By the time she was five, she started paddling in the bay on a 5'2" surfboard that her father cut down from his longboard collection. At age seven she took that same board out in the ocean and got hooked on the stoke of riding waves. Today, Jamie has a quiver of eight boards, ranging from 5'10" to 6'3" and one 9' longboard.

Jamie's competition history is just as amazing. She participated in a local contest sponsored by Surf Unlimited when she was twelve years old. She took second place in that first contest, and then first place the next year. She started surfing regularly in ESA contests after that. She won the Northeast Regionals five times and the Eastern Championships in 2002. Jamie placed second in the U.S. Championships in 1999 and qualified for the U.S. Team in 1999 and 2000.

With corporate sponsorship from names like Local Motion (surfboards), Reef (footwear), Dragon (eyewear) and Ron Jon Surf Shop, Jamie has been able to make the move to surfing in professional contests. She has placed as high as second (Virginia Beach, 2001) and fourth (Cape Hatteras, 2002). Her goal for the future is to compete in as many contests as possible on the Pro Surfing Tour and live her dream to travel and surf. At barely twenty years old, Jamie has already surfed exotic places that most surfers only dream about: Cabo, Costa Rica, Dominican Republic, Argentina, Brazil, Australia, and Hawaii.

* * *

Brendan Willem (SRHS class of 2003) hit the water on a surfboard for the first time when he was five years old. Before that, he remembers "surfing" a pillow and "dropping in" from his mother's couch to the floor while watching ESPN's *Summer Nights* with surfers like Cheyne Horan. Another standout that

Brendan has been watching for quite a while is his father Bill Willem. Bill has been competing since he was fifteen years old and still competes in ESA events up and down the East Coast. Surfing is truly a family love affair in the Willem house with eleven-year-old Conner also taking to the water.

At seventeen, Brendan already has a huge list of accomplishments. He finished first in the 2000 NSSA State Championships in both Men's Shortboard and Longboard competitions and eighth in the ESA's East Coast Championship in 2002. He also participated in the invitation-only First Annual Garden State Grudge Match in 2002. In addition to riding locally for Surf Shack Surf Shop, he has attracted the attention of some big-name sponsors including: Split (apparel), O'Neill (wetsuits), and McCrystal (surfboards). If all that weren't enough, Brendan's picture has already appeared in *Surfer* (2001) and *Surfnews* (2002). Only a small number of surfers, of any age, can boast that kind of visibility.

Despite all his accomplishments, Brendan is surprisingly humble. He remains focused as he pursues dreams of surfing professionally after high school. With his determination and natural instinct in the water, there's no telling how far he will go. By land and by sea, Brendan is a classy kid and a role-model for future SRHS surfers . . . which just may include younger brother Conner.

* * *

A surf team reunion, of sorts, occurred October 2002, with SRHS surfers past and present making an admirable showing. The First Annual Garden State Grudge Match was held in Seaside Heights, organized by Smith Optics. It was an invitation-only event for twenty-four competitors, in nor'easter conditions. Happy to oblige the invitation were LBI'ers: Brendan Willem, Randy Townsend, Justin Citta, and Ben McBrien. Invited, but unable to attend, was Sammy Zuegner. McBrien made it to the semi-finals and faced off against Dean Randazzo. Randazzo is apparently still a nemesis to the SRHS competitors and walked away with the $2,000 purse and bragging rights, but only for one year. You can be sure that our boys will be back next year to give him a run for his money.

(**A**) Randy Townsend (**B**)Ben McBrien (**C**)Justin Citta (**D**)Brendan Willem (**E**) Jamie DeWitt "larger than life" in the front window of Ron Jon Surf Shop in Ship Bottom (**F**) Intraclub Meet 2001 - SRHS Faculty: Craig Henry (principal), Joe Medica (science), Steve Papach (substitute), Darryl Heale (guidance), Tice Ryan (LBTBP), Joanne Rist (art), Tom Ackers (industrial arts), Will Zylinski (history), Barbara Conover (substitute).

References:

Borte, Jason. "Heat Wave: Sweating Out Hurricane Season Along the East Coast." *Surfer* 43(2), 2001, 76-95.

Steele, Jon. "Stormy Affair: The Torrid Relationship between Eastern Surfers and the Atlantic's Annual Hurricane Season." *Surfer* 44(2), 2003, 82-101.

"Exposure." *Surfnews* 4(8), 2002, 46.

Holyoke Avenue Surfers Alliance

In May 1996, the Borough of Beach Haven submitted an *Application for Department of the Army Permit* for the proposed Holyoke Avenue Groin Modification project. "Groin modification" sounds pretty painful, but what really caught the attention of some local surfers was the "Holyoke Avenue" part.

Holyoke Avenue is known for a break, that, when the conditions are right, rivals any break on the island, perhaps on the East Coast. So, you can see why some people would be upset with anything that would change that. At 202 feet, the Holyoke jetty is one of the largest on the island. It has been blamed by many for the erosion problems between Holyoke and Iroquois Avenues. According to the Army Corps of Engineers public notice, the proposed modifications would "remove a seventy-three foot section of the jetty's upper layer of rocks, four to five feet in height, to the approximate mean low water line." Proponents of the notch felt it would alleviate erosion problems south of the jetty by allowing the sand to naturally migrate down the coast instead of being "trapped" by the jetty.

A group of approximately thirty individuals from the local community opposed the project. This group of surfers, fishermen, Beach Haven homeowners, and local business owners formed a non-profit, unincorporated association known as the Holyoke Avenue Surfers Alliance. It didn't hurt that the key founders of the group had legal expertise and knowledge of "wave science."

Included in this group were : Betsy Wurzburg, a former Washington, D.C., federal attorney and longtime resident of Beach Haven; Albert Gomez, a local businessman and twenty-five year Holyoke surfing veteran; John Ryan, a local surfer and New Jersey attorney who also provides legal representation for the New Jersey chapter of the Surfrider Foundation; and Ric Anastasi, who in addition to being a surfer (currently owns Ric's Aloha Classics in Beach Haven), was also a former lifeguard at the Holyoke Beach for eight years. Ric's lifesaving background made him an important player when it came time to explain the menacing currents and their threat to public safety. Ric's address became the headquarters for the association because of his close proximity to Holyoke Avenue.

Betsy remembers that the Alliance was really a ragtag group of individuals with diverse backgrounds. The jetty issue brought together a combination of white-haired homeowners established in the community, and energetic young people who were beach badge checkers and surfers. Together they attended meetings and combed the beaches for petition signatures. A mutual respect grew out of their shared efforts and lasting friendships were formed.

The group hit the ground, or shall we say beach, running, early in July 1996. Written comments were submitted to the Army Corps of Engineers objecting to the proposed notching project and requesting a public hearing on the matter. Additional letters were written to lobby congressional support.

Petitions were circulated in the community in a way that delineated the multiple concerns of multiple groups. All along it was important that this not just be considered an issue of the surfers against the establishment. The residents, taxpayers, and summer visitors signed one petition which voiced concerns about "recreational use, safety, and the economic and environmental infrastructure." Homeowners north of the jetty would play an important role verbalizing their concerns about the notch merely jeopardizing one beach for another, and placing their homes in peril. There was also the issue of expense. While the Federal Emergency Management Agency (FEMA) had already approved the hazard mitigation grant for $100,000, contingent on Army Corps permit to begin, the project was estimated to cost $200,000. That brought up questions about a bond issue from taxpayers. There was also a question of who would foot the bill for any additional expenses: storing the removed rocks, replacing them if the notching was deemed unsuccessful, baseline and monitoring studies on the effects of the project.

The fishermen petitioned that their recreational use of the Holyoke jetty would be prohibited by unsafe conditions. The notch would prevent individuals from safely walking to the end. Those who did walk out on a low tide, might become trapped as the tide came in. It was also felt that the natural habitat of the fish in this unique location might be disrupted by the new configuration as well as the equipment needed to do the excavation.

The surfers made their point not only on the recreational impact but also for the severe hazard to swimmers and surfers on both sides of the jetty. The fear was that the notch would create a funnel through the jetty, resulting in much stronger and faster currents. It would also move all currents closer to the beach where swimmers would be caught unaware of the change in conditions. The hidden field of rocks would add additional safety concerns.

When all was said and done, over a thousand signatures were obtained on these combined petitions. The Holyoke Avenue Surfers Alliance had raised enough interest that the Army Corps of Engineers consented to an informal workshop in Beach Haven on September 26, 1996. There were several hours of discussion between borough commissioners, engineers, surfers in suits, and impassioned homeowners from both sides of the jetty.

The mood of the crowd began to swing in favor of the Alliance as their familiarity with the ocean began to be seen as an asset. These locals, as they made their case for the borough's well-being, were proving themselves to be experts in their community. They were as equally, if not more informed, than the "outside" experts, some of whom had never even seen the jetty. Many of the surfers voiced concerns about everything from public safety to lack of field data, and the exorbitant expenditure for something that might not even work. John Ryan, a legal representative of the New Jersey chapter of the Surfrider Foundation, took a militant surfer line and boldly went on the record to say, "I'm not ashamed to stand here and say I'm concerned over the quality of the surf at Holyoke Avenue. It's not unprecedented in the United States for a wave to be considered a valuable natural resource . . . I would like to see the issue addressed as to what happens to that wave."

Both sides waited to hear the Army Corps' decision that came on Nov.19, 1996. The Army Corps sent a letter to the borough engineer requesting several items in order to "continue processing" the application. Data were still needed to predict the success of the notching project. The Borough would also have to develop a beach monitoring program. Finally, there would have to be "an assessment of the effects that the project would have on existing surfing conditions at the Holyoke Avenue beach," including a "hydrographic survey of the nearshore ocean bottom both north and south of the groin." Who would ever have guessed that the Army Corps of Engineers would have been interested in surfing conditions? In fact, this study ordered by the Army Corps would probably have cost more than the project itself. That helped kill the proposal. In a modern-day David and Goliath story, news came on December 12, 1996 that the Borough of Beach Haven had withdrawn their request for a permit.

Thanks to the well-organized and persistent efforts of the Holyoke Avenue Surfers Alliance, far from being beach bums, surfers were acknowledged as being pivotal players in the successful resolution of this problem. The following winter, significant erosion occurred on the north side of Holyoke jetty due to tremendous north to south surges. Had the jetty been notched, there is the strong possibility that property would have been lost on the north side. Ultimately, the right decision had been made, and it wasn't all about surfing, as some skeptics had suspected.

Nevertheless, when all was said and done, the locally-loved surf break had been preserved. This break was later captured for the whole world to see when "The Best East Coast Tube Ever Seen," was featured in the international magazine, *Surfer* in 2001. Against all odds, the Holyoke wave still breaks, thanks to the tremendous efforts of the Holyoke Avenue Surfers Alliance.

References:

Application for Department of the Army Permit (33 CFR 325). Borough of Beach Haven (May 22, 1996).

Borte, Jason. Heat Wave: Sweating out hurricane season along the East Coast." *Surfer* 43(2), 2001, 76-95.

Mellerup, Rick. "Surfers Riding Wave of Momentum in Fight Against Notching Jetty." *The SandPaper* (August 28, 1996): 20 & 26.

Petition for a Public Hearing in the Matter of the Proposed Modification of the Holyoke Avenue Jetty. Holyoke Avenue Surfers Alliance (July, 1996).

*Public Notice (*CENAP-OP-R-199502465-42*).* U.S. Army Corps of Engineers—Philadelphia District (July 2,1996).

Shinn, R.C. (New Jersey State Commissioner- Department of Environmental Protection).
"Official Letter to Legislators" (December 12, 1996).

Statement prepared for workshop meeting among interested parties at Beach Haven Borough Hall. Holyoke Avenue Surfers Alliance (September 26, 1996).

New Jersey Surf Club

The first New Jersey Surf Club (NJSC) Meeting took place in February 2001. This non-profit organization has been attracting members ever since from New Jersey, New York, and Pennsylvania. The meetings have been scattered throughout several towns on Long Beach Island. Meetings are a combination of surfing, eating, and business discussion.

It goes without saying that the amount of work that gets accomplished is inversely proportional to how good the surf is. Nevertheless, a lot has been accomplished in a short amount of time. The NJSC has lent its support in several areas. A representative from the club was in touch with the mayor of Cape May when a proposed Surf Camp in that town was jeopardized. The NJSC was also contacted via Internet to prevent the closing of a surfing beach in Maine. Combined with input from individual surfers and clubs throughout the country, this beach closing was prevented.

The NJSC is also prepared to take a strong stand on environmental issues. All members were kept informed of two important issues recently. One of these was the proposed ocean dumping off of Sandy Hook at the Historic Area Remediation Site (HARS). Another issue is the strong correlation between the U.S. Navy's use of Low Frequency Active Sonar and marine mammal strandings and deaths throughout the world. In addition to club members being urged to individually contact the appropriate agencies, a copy of the club's position statement was sent to the editor of every newspaper in New Jersey to raise awareness and rally support.

The overall success of the NJSC is due in great part to Barry Schwartz who had the idea for the club and has been spearheading the efforts ever since. Barry didn't actually start surfing until he was fifty. Growing up, he spent a lot of time in Atlantic City, but never saw anyone surfing there. Though he has always loved the ocean, it was his desire to spend more time with his son that actually got him out on a surfboard. Now at fifty-four, it's hard to keep him out of the surf. When he's not riding surfboards he's also collecting them. His enthusiasm bubbles over into the NJSC. He sees the club as a way for "people to be together who wouldn't normally be together and just have fun."

People don't need to be intimidated if they don't surf well or don't know all the "lingo." That's the farthest thing on anyone's mind. The club gives people an immediate network for carpooling to LBI, traveling abroad, trading and selling equipment, or just sharing water time and surf stories. NJSC is also planning "fun" surf meets (nothing too serious) and hopes to lend support to some community fundraisers. Click on *www.NJSC.org* to find out more.

Home page of the New Jersey Surf Club - *www.NJSC.org*

Local Boards

One of the earliest board builders on Long Beach Island was undoubtedly **Stretch Pohl**. Stretch's first board was one that he purchased in 1932, directly from Tom Blake in California. Soon after, Stretch tried building these 12' to14' hollow monsters himself. Stretch would go on to build surfboards through every phase of board development, from the hollow wooden to 7' fiberglass designs.

Stretch and Tom Blake kept in contact through the years, sharing their vision of surfing. Tom had quite a vision to share. He is considered to be one of the most influential figures in modern surfing for inventions such as the first hollow surfboard, first sailboard, and first waterproof camera housing to be used for surfing. Tom also experimented with bottom rockers, tail configurations, and was the first person to put a fin on a surfboard.

Stretch was initially attracted to Blake's paddleboard for its application in the lifesaving arena. Stretch, who was a National Red Cross Director in North Jersey, introduced it to be used as part of their standard equipment. Stretch later taught classes about ocean lifesaving, promoting the use of this hollow wooden paddleboard.

The lifesaving board was only the beginning. A group of about six watermen, known as the Malolo Akula Surfboard Club, actually rode the waves on their own hand-made hollow boards in the 1930s. Their unofficial headquarters was Wright's Pier on 20th Street in Ship Bottom. Don't look for that pier now - it was destroyed in the 1944 Hurricane.

The next boards that hit the scene were the balsa-redwood composites. They were first used in California in the late 1930s.

Stretch promoted a composite board known as the Larronde Model in the mid-1940s. The information sheet that Stretch distributed about this board was of too poor a quality to be reproduced for this book. Instead, the text has been reproduced below. This board was attractive due to the inclusion of balsa wood. Balsa made them lighter than the hollow redwood boards. Redwood was still used in crucial areas (stringer, rails, nose and tail blocks) to provide greater durability.

JOHN E.O. LARRONDE'S MORRISSEY SHAPE REDWOOD-BALSA BOARD

My good friend from the West Coast forwards to me a sketch of a solid board which is the latest rage among the surfriders out there.

The dimensions are four inches by twenty-two inches by one hundred and forty-four inches. The weight of the board is 106 lbs. dry. The balsa is arranged so that it lies in the center of the board with the redwood furnishing the nose blocks and sides. I have been fortunate enough to secure the lumber required for such a board and I hope that by the time the Maluhia Surf Club June clinic is held, you will be able to give 'er a try. From all reports, John tells me this model rides very well in any type of water which is something we've all been looking for. Possibly in the fall I shall give a detailed account of the performance of the board in our eastern waters. The sketch below is not to scale and lacks fundamental details. However, if you're interested in building one, I'll be glad to furnish you with the plans.

This is a surfriding board designed for one man. The wood is glued together in long strips and then the entire board is hand-worked to shape. You will note the board requires a fin which can be made of wood or metal. This gives you direction and prevents skidding of the board once you make contact with a wave. The "plank" as they call them, is varnished with a good marine product.

They say 3 coats well-sanded in between applications is a must . . . we agree. Wood must be obtained from the West Coast and the entire board plus milling charges should cost you in the vicinity of $35.00. Tom Blake informs me that his 14 footer which will support two riders is now available . . . just like my Pilikea . . . price $90.00 with special discounts for you.

- "Stretch" Pohl

Both the hollow and the composite wooden boards were treated with a "good marine product." Progress in surfboard design took a huge leap when fiberglass and resin replaced varnish. Bob Simmons from California was the first to make fiberglass balsa surfboards in 1949. The combination of fiberglass fabric and liquid resin around solid balsa yielded a lighter and stronger board. The average weight of surfboards was cut in half without compromising the tensile strength of the board.

The actual birth of the surfboard industry, however, was not until the early 1960s with the introduction of polyurethane foam. Foam had several intrinsic advantages and was also more readily available. While wooden boards required tedious sanding along the grain of the wood, foam was easily shaped with several sweeps of the sander. In the case of the "pop-out" surfboard, a foam blank came out of a mold, already closely approximating the board's shape with only minimal sanding required. "Custom" boards were created by gluing two pieces of foam on either side of a wooden stringer and then shaping as desired. Even boards with finer details like nose and tail blocks were still less labor-intensive than the wooden boards that required the gluing of multiple separate pieces of wood.

Polyurethane also contrasted with balsa in terms of longevity. Balsa, because it was so fibrous, immediately soaked up water with even the smallest dings. Any moisture would then be carried throughout the length of the board, eventually destroying the integrity of the wood and making it heavier. Another consideration was that balsa had to be imported from

South America and was not readily available. When the potential for the polyurethane foam was realized, several companies sprang up in California in the 1960s. Among these were companies like: Foss, Walker, and Clark. The wide availability of polyurethane opened the door for surfboards to be produced on a larger scale than ever before.

The lightness in weight afforded by polyurethane foam made it much more appealing and manageable for the average person. The average person also knew a little bit more about surfing by now. There was ever increasing media attention. The movie "Gidget," was released in 1959, based on the best-selling book by Fritz Kohner. A 1962 issue of *Popular Mechanics* had information about surfboard building. People who had never even seen the ocean were tapping their feet to the Beach Boys' "Surfin USA." That song hit #3 on the Billboard charts in March 1963.

Meanwhile, on Long Beach Island in 1961, one of the first things you saw when you drove over the Causeway was the Ron Jon trailer with large lettering that simply said: SURF BOARDS. By the mid-1960s several individuals were building surfboards commercially on the island including: Frank Acuff -Acuff Surfboards (North Beach Haven) and Biff Barrett - Biff's Custom Boards (Ship Bottom). Just on the other side of the bridge was Wimpy Paulsworth at the Clam Stand in Manahawkin.

* * *

Dozens of others were trying to build their own boards. **Ralph Bourgeois**, one of the early presidents of the LBI Surfing Association, was one of them. His son, Rick, remembers him "building boards for the entire family." Rick was fortunate because by the time it came time for him to get his board as the youngest, his father had figured out some of the finer points of board-building. They never did figure out the ventilation thing, though. They had several canaries that were family pets that mysteriously died, undoubtedly from the resin fumes.

Finding all the necessary supplies for surfboard construction was a feat in itself in the early days. At first, Ralph had to rely on boat resins and even used foam that was intended for insulation in walk-in refrigerators. He glued foam pieces together that were typically three to four inches thick and six feet long. Eventually, more supplies became available at Ron Jon's Surf Shop.

Rick recalls the time that his father was "determined to build a board with rocker like the ones that were coming out of California." Ralph borrowed a Hobie surfboard from a friend and had his oldest son hold the surfboard straight in front of him like he was holding a tray of food. He took a picture of the rail and then converted the proportions on to a ten foot piece of graph paper. The graph paper was tacked onto a redwood stringer so that the stringer could be cut to the exact proportions with a jig. Polyurethane foam was glued on either side of the stringer as usual, and foam sanded down until it conformed to the shape of the stringer. It was a lengthy process, but it worked. Back then, everyone was still inventing the wheel.

* * *

Richard Lisiewski was one of the first LBI'ers to build surfboards on a large scale. He set-up a 4,000 square-foot factory on the mainland in Riverside, New Jersey. Richard manufactured close to 3,000 custom and pop-out surfboards, wakeboards, and belly boards from 1962 to1966. He made boards for his own labels - Collier (custom) and Matador (pop-out). Richard was also contracted to make boards for shop labels like Curcio (Curcio Surf Shop in Atlantic City), and Wave Master (Mogul's Surf Shop in Clifton).

Richard's boards achieved national attention when the Sherry and Harrington (S&H) Green Stamp Company placed one of his boards in their redemption catalog. (For all you youngsters, a dollar amount of grocery bills earned "x" amount of stamps). His Collier surfboard could be redeemed for 30,000 points. In another unique opportunity, Eastman Kodak used a Matador surfboard in one of their advertisements featured at Grand Central Station in New York City.

Richard left surfboard manufacturing for the surfing retail business, where he has been ever since. While working in retail, Richard became acquainted with another surfboard builder, Dan Heritage. Richard graciously showed Dan some of the finer points of board building when Dan was starting out. "It wasn't long after that," Richard recalls, "that he got really good." (Dan was recognized at the Inaugural East Coast Surf Legends Hall of Fame in 1996).

Richard's Matador and Collier surfboards and decals are sought after by collectors today. Some of them appear in surfing museums in California, Hawaii, and Australia.

* * *

Only a youngster when much of this was happening, **Roger Holden**, would go on to be an innovator in surfboard design. He remembers using a fourteen foot cedar board as a young teenager, and then the fiberglass boards that became the standard. He was a respected competitor in mid-Atlantic surfing events. Roger finished first in the Long Beach Island Championship in 1968 and in the top three in the East Coast Championships in 1967, 1969, 1970.

Roger operated Island East Surfboards by Holden Shop in Harvey Cedars from 1966 to 1974. He estimates that he built approximately 350 surfboards for the 'Island East' label. In the early 70s, Roger began experimenting with a 6' square tail design with vee bottom and thin rails, as well as other innovative "short" board deigns. Roger later teamed up with Pat McGrath in 1997 to build Island East surfboards in Manahawkin.

Roger is very proud he passed on his love of surfing to his sons. He sees the sport as a positive influence on character development. He continues to surf although his days of competition ended long ago. During the finals of a meet held in Asbury Park, he simply paddled in, coming to the realization that he was at the contest surfing for others, and not for himself. These days, Roger intentionally shys away from any publicity. Surfing for him carries the greatest meaning in its spirituality. "When you're out there its something between you and the waves and God. It's not for the recognition."

* * *

Vince Balas and his *Planet Blue* surfboards represent the future generations of surfboard design and production. Vince, a Forked River native, started this line of boards during the winter of 1983 in San Clemente, California where he still has a factory producing boards.

Vince's initial exposure to surfboard production was through Long Beach Surf and Ski. This shop was located on the Causeway and Barnegat Avenue in Ship Bottom - the former home of Rick Surf Shop. Vince worked the retail aspect, ding repair, and later helped the shop's owner, Michael Cole, build boards for the Inner Motion label. When Vince traveled to California, right out of high school, he started to get a feel for who some of the best shapers were on the West Coast. He convinced a talented shaper named Randy Sleigh, (contract shaper for companies like *Pacific Designs* and *Aloha*), to build him two boards. The condition was, however, that Vince would get to watch him shape the whole time. This was Vince's opportunity to pay attention to the finer details, like wings and channels, and to ask questions. Vince also spent some time on the North Shore of Hawaii at the *Island Classic* factory, picking up some more pointers from Eric Arakawa.

Learning from some of the best paid off for Vince. Surf shops carry *Planet Blue* surfboards from New York to Delaware, and in California and Puerto Rico. Vince estimates that he has produced close to 10,000 boards to date. Vince has a big following in the Seaside, Belmar, and Pt. Pleasant areas from the days when Grog's Surf Palace in Seaside carried his line of boards. Since Grog's closed, Right Coast in Seaside has taken over the line. Of course, you can also find his boards on LBI in Ron Jon Surf Shop, Surf Shack, and Jonathan Law Studio.

Vince builds stock boards as well as custom boards to the surfer's specifications. Each year, Vince develops two to three new designs that he lets his team members try to get feedback. Once everyone is satisfied, he hand shapes the blank and then lets the world of high-technology take over. He scans information from nose to tail about one half of the board - stringer to rail. Everything is considered—the width of the board, thickness of the rails, concaves, etc. The computer then creates a mirror image which insures symmetry to within 1/100th of an inch.

The program data sheet that is created about the surfboard is sent to a quarter million dollar machine in Carlsbad, California. This machine locks in a surfboard blank and cuts away at the foam, reproducing what the computer knows as Vince's hand-shaped design. The end result is less human error and a much greater volume. The machine is capable of cutting 500 surfboards per week and is presently being used by twenty-plus surfboard companies across the country.

Vince still has to smooth out the ripples in the preliminary blanks shaped by the computer. He also adds his own touch re-shaping the nose and tail where the foam blank is intentionally left thicker for the machine to hold it into place. Nevertheless, Vince's shaping time is reduced at least seventy-five percent for what is typically the most labor intensive portion of the board building process.

Anyone interested in finding out more about *Planet Blue* surfboards can call the factory at (609) 693-7062. Vince will open a surf shop next to his factory location during the Summer of 2003 at 424 Main Street (Route 9) in West Creek. It will feature a "mass quantity of boards—short and long," core clothing—baggies, swimsuits, *Planet Blue* clothing, and hard goods—leashes, track top, and wax. You'll want to check it out!

* * *

Bill Kretzer started surfing LBI when he was nine years old and was fixing surfboards by the time he was fourteen. The skilled hands of a craftsman and a keen eye for hydrodynamic lines were already in his blood. Bill comes from a long line of wooden boat builders. The family business was Kretzer Boat Works from 1906 to 1976.

It seemed to be a natural choice for Bill to combine his passion for surfing with what he found to be a natural talent for building boards. He refined his skills, reading everything he could from shapers like Maurice Cole, Simon Anderson, and Rusty Preisendorfer. Bill wasn't afraid to experiment with different contours and fin placements. It was trial and error for a few years until he decided to produce his own line of boards in 1990 - *Home Grown*. Conflict over the name, which was also being used by a board manufacturer in Hawaii, resulted in the *Kretzer* line of boards shortly after that. These boards are sold today in shops from Rhode Island to Maryland. Bill has shaped hundreds of boards over the years, specializing in performance shortboards, fish, and fun boards.

You can check out his boards locally at Beach Nutz Surf Shop, or find out more at his website, *www.Kretzersurfboards.com*. This site will also give more information about upcoming manuals Bill has been working on about shaping and glassing techniques, as well as specialty shaping tools. Bill will be happy to provide technical support for would-be board builders at an e-mail address to be specified in the manuals.

* * *

Skip Miller is another surfer with strong Long Beach Island connections who has traveled the world in search of waves. What makes Skip unique is that he is known by the surfing community around the world. Our story actually begins in Ocean City, New Jersey where Skip's parents had a summer home. A native of the Bryn Mawr, Pennsylvania area, Skip was introduced to surfing on the Jersey shore when he was about fourteen. His love affair with LBI began the first time he surfed Harvey Cedars in 1980.

Skip stumbled upon Long Beach Surf and Ski in Ship Bottom out of necessity one day. He was trying to get his board fixed quickly to salvage the rest of the day's surf. That day he met and formed lasting friendships with Mike Cole, who owned the shop, and Vince Balas who was helping him build the *Inner Motion* line of boards. By this time, Skip was already recognized as a talented Eastern Surfing Association (ESA) surfer and was sponsored by Heritage Surfboards. Mike would eventually offer to build a Skip Miller signature board known as the 'Checkerboard Series.' The bigger thrill for Skip, however, was when Cole gave Skip the go-ahead to personally shape his own surfboard.

At the end of that summer, Skip proudly placed his handiwork on the roof of his car for his return trip to college in California. Somewhere on the interstate highway in Arizona, the board blew off the roof. Skip frantically got on his C.B. radio and started asking truckers if they had seen any surfboard debris on the road. Skip finally found the board. He was still determined to ride his "own board" in California waters. That he did, even though the symmetrics of the board had changed significantly. Skip remembers that if it wasn't for the skegs, it would have been difficult to distinguish the nose from the tail at that point.

Skip attended the University of California in San Diego. His roommates were none other than Rob Gilley (Photo Editor for *The Surfer's Journal*) and John Bilderback (Senior Photographer *Surfer*). At the time, Rob and John were collaborating as part of *Choice Photos*. They succeeded in capturing the same surfing moments with Rob taking shots by land and John by water. Skip readily admits that they were "surf junkies" back then. From their San Diego apartment they made regular trips to places like Malibu, Tressles, and Baja.

While Rob and John were consumed with their photography, Skip was building as many boards as he could, mainly for his friends. The board recipients would pay all the costs of the materials and Skip offered free labor in return for valuable experience. Rob Gilley was the one who coined the label for Skip's boards: *Line Drive*.

Skip returned to the East Coast with plans to purchase Long Beach Surf and Ski. When Mike Cole decided to hold onto his shop a little longer, Skip instead opened a new store in Harvey Cedars that he called Line Drive Surf Shop (1982-1985). In order to provide his own line of custom boards, he opened a factory in Manahawkin. From there, Skip did the shaping and teamed up with Vince Balas to do the glassing. Line Drive Surf Shop sold a collection of baggies, t-shirts, accessories (leashes,wax, etc.), boogie boards, and of course, Line Drive Surfboards.

Skip's next business venture was with John Bealle. You may recognize the name Bealle from Bealle's Shop N' Bag—now

Murphy's Market. Beach Haven Surf & Sport, located at 7 South Bay Avenue, was unique because there was a shaping room in the store. It was sound-proofed and had a glass window so customers could watch Skip at work. Skip then purchased Y-Knot Surf Shop (8 Long Beach Boulevard, Surf City) from Robby Batista. Skip later bought out Bealle's investment in Beach Haven Surf & Sport and changed the name of the Beach Haven store to Y-Knot Surf Shop as well.

During this time period, Skip began wintering in Hawaii and shaping for well-known companies like Hawaiian Island Creations and Rusty. Skip even had a six-month stint in Australia. That's where Terry Fitzgerald gave him the opportunity to shape for Hot Buttered with the ultimatum: "Make four boards, if they sell you can keep going." Skip worked his way up from sweeping the floor and ding repair to having all the work he could handle, sometimes six days a week. Skip says he was sorry when his VISA ran out and he had to leave Australia.

Skip was also finding it increasingly harder to leave Hawaii and return to his business responsibilities in New Jersey. He closed the two New Jersey-based shops in 1988 and opened a Y-Knot Surf Shop in Honolulu instead. Skip also lived and worked with Eric Arakawa when Eric owned Island Classics Surfboards. Skip handled most of the orders for boards 6'6" and under, as well as all the East Coast accounts. Skip readily admits that Eric is a "master craftsman" and one of the finest shapers of our time. Skip reports, "It was always a humbling experience to put one of your boards on the rack next to his."

Don't let that statement fool you. Skip is pretty accomplished himself, even shaping for two world-class surfers. He shaped a Hawaiian Island Creation for Bryce Ellis when he was ranked sixteenth in the world. He remembers "sweating bullets" when Bryce Ellis came in the shaping room to see how his board was progressing. He also shaped a Rusty 6'2" thruster for the sixth ranked, Bob Bain. Skip can still picture its flat deck that was only 18" wide with 2" rails. When looking back on that whole experience, Skip admits that he "never expected to get this far -

that some kid from New Jersey would have the opportunity to shape for such world-class surfers."

Skip's next adventure took him to Puerto Rico where he lived until 2000. He had some small factories in Puerto Rico where he primarily shaped guns. Since this location was a little off the beaten track for a shaper, he supplemented his income running the *Tres Palmas Inn,* catering to surfers. He even played guitar in a local band known as *Bedrock.* Since the summers are a dry season for waves in Puerto Rico, Skip used that time for surf trips to places like Mexico and Indonesia. He also made treks back to New Jersey to catch up with family and friends.

When there are no waves to be found, Skip has also enjoyed sailing. He was a formidable opponent racing sailboats when he was in Hawaii at Kona. Skip points out the strong similarities between the two sports: waves, water, and wind. The sailing is challenging in a different way. "It is like a chess match on the water." Skip enjoys the tactical nature of the sport and "needing to use your mind to succeed."

Skip's love for the sport of sailing eventually influenced him to teach it. Since 2000, Skip has even been traveling back to LBI in the summer to assist with the Youth Sailing Program at Barnegat Light Yacht Club (actually in Harvey Cedars). Skip is especially proud of leading his group of thirteen to fifteen year old boys in national competition. This group finished tenth in the nation at the 2002 Sear's Cup held at Annapolis, Maryland. This is even more amazing since this group of young men was competing against primarily seventeen and eighteen year olds.

These days, Skip is still shaping Line Drive Surfboards and is living in Jacksonville, Florida, although he has plans to move back to Hawaii. He is joined by his wife Jackie, nine-year-old daughter Brianna, and eighteen-month-old son Noah. They are happy to announce that another son is on the way.

Of surfing Skip says, *"It has been an intense passion and great experience for over 25 years."* Locally, you can find Skip's boards at Farias Surf Shop on LBI and also at No Flat Earth in Brick and Forked River.

* * *

Paul Boardman is a native of Australia who started coming to LBI ten years ago. That's when a friend got him connected working as a lifeguard at Long Beach Township Beach Patrol for the summer. He knew he couldn't fulfill his dream of traveling without working, so it was a perfect match to get to the states. It began what Paul considers, "Five and a half years of an 'Endless Summer,' or eleven consecutive summers." Paul got the opportunity to surf in warm water all year-round. He enjoyed the LBI summer season and then traveled back to Australia in time for their summer, often by way of places like South Africa and Hawaii for more surfing opportunities.

Paul was initially impressed by the "level of surfing" he witnessed from some of our LBI locals. Paul is a good judge when it comes to that. He has several Aussie friends who are professional surfers. Paul was also part of the water safety crew at several professional surfing world events in Australia. In Paul's own words, some of our locals are "right up there."

What else did Paul notice about LBI? When he moved to Barnegat Light year-round to pursue commercial fishing, he was abruptly introduced to our "harsh environment, with winters so cold and summers so short." He says it took him a good three years to really get comfortable with winter surfing. He still remembers early-on, attempting to stand up on several critical take-offs and "tripping over my booties . . . I kept catching the front of my foot . . . I just wasn't accustomed to it."

When the fishing business falls off in the summer time, Paul supplements his income repairing surfboards, giving surf lessons, and even building a few boards under his label: *Boardman*. (With a name like 'Boardman,' how could you go wrong?) Paul originally started making boards "that suited me and then made some for friends." Paul builds all shapes and sizes but being over two hundred pounds himself, he understands how to build a high performance board for "big guys." You can reach him at 361-9686 if you have any special requests. This mate from 'down under' knows his surfing.

Original image from the S&H Green Stamps catalogue picturing a Collier surfboard that was available for redemption. Surfboard logos from some other local manufacturers are included.

Local Breaks

The following information was collected from input from a number of individuals, familiar with their local breaks. For fear of retaliation, all have requested to maintain their anonymity. Let's face it though, none of this is really a secret and it's subject to change with the next big nor'easter.

Keep in mind the following things when you're selecting an LBI break:

1) The waves aren't always bigger on someone else's beach. Check your break first—you may be pleasantly surprised.
2) The key factors that you'll need to bear in mind for predicting wave conditions are: ground swell, present wind direction, tide schedule and how that correlates with the bottom conditions and location of jetties on different LBI beaches.
3) If your skills don't match the conditions you're seeing—Watch from the beach! Don't be a threat to yourself or to others. Being a menace in the water is one sure way to get the "locals" upset with you.
4) Rules about all day surfing beaches are subject to change at the discretion of the municipality. Beaches are guarded the weekend before July 4th through Labor Day, between the hours of 10 A.M. and 5 P.M. Some towns allow surfing outside the designated swimmers' area. Ask the lifeguard on your beach what the rules are. If there is no guard (township borders or sparsely populated areas), you probably won't get hassled, but don't quote me.

5) In-season, you'll need the respective town's beach badge to get on the beach. Once you're in the water, the beach badge checkers won't come after you. Public restrooms are also seasonal and are locked in the off-season.

Moving from north to south, LBI surfers have some of the following choices:

ISLAND BEACH STATE PARK

Pecker Heads (bottom conditions have the appearance of a bird's beak from overhead) This area is just north of Barnegat Inlet. It is frequently visited by LBI surfers by boat who anchor off the sandbar. It is also within reach of the LBI surfer by paddling across the inlet although you should know that there is a dangerous current and lots of boat traffic. Consequently, the Coast Guard frowns on this and can fine perpetrators up to $500 for "obstruction of a waterway." It breaks well with a south swell.

BARNEGAT LIGHT

12th Street shoals—This is traditionally *a longboard or funboard spot* with long rolling lefts when the conditions are right—it tends to be fickle. Recently with changing sandbars, probably due to the new jetty configuration, there is a steeper inside section which is making it more attractive to shortboarders as well. It breaks best on a strong southeast ground swell. It's the longest paddle on the island and there are also strong currents at work here. You need to be an experienced paddler and strong swimmer for this break. On a south swell paddle out around 15th Street and drift into position.

22nd-23rd Streets—This is Barnegat Light's shortboard spot of choice

LOVELADIES

This area is normally uncrowded. Most beaches are private so unless you know someone, you have no choice but to park at the public access between the church and tennis courts. From there, choose your break on foot. There are some unguarded beaches during the summer. Beware of private property.

HARVEY CEDARS

The wave of choice at the north end. The area is known for its own breed of locals. It's shallow sandbars create a steeper wave. This wave will still break when other spots are too deep.

Coffee Shop—80th Street

Toilet Bowl at Bergen Avenue—Many surfing contests are held here. The slogan here is "Make the bowl or get flushed," although the break seems to be mellowing with time.

Hudson Avenue—This break tends to be crowded and very localized. There is more than ample parking on the street by the ocean and especially across the boulevard at Sunset Park. This park on the bayside runs the length of Salem, Hudson, and Passaic Avenues. The park has public restrooms, showers, playground equipment, picnic area, and a small sailboat launch area. It's also a good choice for launching wind surfers. In other words, if the people you're traveling with don't surf, they can still keep amused here.

NORTH BEACH

This is another private area. It is typically less crowded, with some unguarded beaches during the summer. You can use a public access area at the tennis courts (Thank goodness for tennis courts). There's a decent break one beach north that you can get to on foot.

SURF CITY

25th Street—This break is on the North Beach/Surf City border. There is fairly consistent surf here, with more size than the surrounding breaks.

SHIP BOTTOM

8th to 10th Street or 7/11 Beach—This is a spot of choice for day visitors because of it's easy on and off the island. Unfortunately, this can also make it pretty crowded. You'll find a lot of beginner surfers here who are accommodated by the easy wave. This spot has historically also been the site of many surfing contests.

28th to 31st Street—Falling on the Brant Beach/Ship Bottom border, this spot can attract a small crowd. Since it is unclaimed by beach patrols from either municipality it is an all-day surfing beach. This break does well with a south swell.

BEGINS FIVE MILES OF CONTINUOUSLY GUARDED BEACHES IN LONG BEACH TOWNSHIP

68th Street—The waves here aren't anything out of the ordinary, but the spot offers some other nice amenities. There is a handicap-accessible observation deck that affords opportunities for great viewing and photography. There are a few public parking spaces, oceanside, by the deck, and more substantial parking west of the boulevard at Bayside Park. For you cross-over water enthusiasts, this park is the windsurfer's spot of choice. Bayside Park also has showers, bathrooms, picnic area, and playground for the rugrats.

BEACH HAVEN CREST

80th Street/ "The Boneyard" is coincidentally also known as Surf Avenue. It's mostly locals. The break is known for its funneling action and extra wave size.

BEACH HAVEN PARK

106th Street has one of the larger jetties on the island. The south side breaks well on a north swell. On the right day, it can give you the feel of a point break. It tends to be a less crowded break.

BEACH HAVEN

10th Street to Taylor Avenue—This area can get pretty crowded. There is public parking oceanside and a lot more parking bayside at the Bay Village/Schooner's Wharf Complex. There is a lot of tourist activity and congestion in this whole area. The pay-off is there are public restrooms, lots of food places to pick from, a playground, and the island's only amusement park within walking distance. If you have to surf all day you don't have to feel guilty about leaving family and friends—there is plenty for them to do. This break seems to attract beginners and experts equally.

Center Street, with ample oceanside parking was once voted the "hippest place to hang out with your surfboard." Part of the attraction is the beachfront eateries and bars (Sea Shell and Engleside). This is the place to be seen if you and your board are just out for a ride. If you do happen to get wet, there are public restrooms and showers here as well.

Berkeley Street is your one chance to shoot the pier (not recommended). There are 3 ½ pilings remain of a fishing pier destroyed in the '44 Hurricane.

Holyoke / "The Oak" is one of the best lefthanders on the island. It breaks best on a north swell and can be spectacular when it goes west or northwest. This is a good place to see some of the local talent all in one place. It's not recommended for beginners. It can get very crowded and is very local.

Leeward Avenue/Nelson Avenue always has a unique break. It's never the biggest but it is a consistently fun spot. There is a public parking lot at the beach and more parking across the boulevard at the ball field. That's where you'll also find some bathrooms and a playground area. It tends to have a short paddle out. You'll find a little bit of an older crowd with an assortment of boards as well as skills at this break.

HOLGATE
(Back to LONG BEACH TOWNSHIP)

First Beach is one beach north of the wooden jetty. There is consistently good surf here, typically lefts. It can get some significant size. You may find surf here when nothing else is breaking.

Wooden Jetty / "The Coffin" affords long lefts past the rockpile and into the cove. It breaks on a north swell and especially when the wind goes west or northwest. It can break a little like a point break with some long lefthanders here. You may consider paddling north of the wooden jetty and drifting into position. Beware 75 yards from the wooden jetty is a rock jetty which can be submerged at times. From there you are jetty free until the end of the preserve. Be sure not to disturb the piping plovers—rangers are watching.

CAPE MAY

During a nor'easter, when the waves are showing some size but are still disorganized and basically unsurfable, you may consider a road trip. The southern tip of Cape May curves enough to make it almost offshore for a cleaner break. It'll be crowded but worth it if you can't wait for things to calm down here.

Local Breaks: (**A**) Barnegat Light shoals (**B**) Bob Nugent in Harvey Cedars, 1985 (**C**) Chris Comfort at 7-11 Beach (**D**) 68th Street coastal monitoring apparatus (**E**) Mark Grasso at Surf Avenue (**F**) Ric Anastasi at Holyoke (**G**) Michael Lisiewski at Wooden Jetty

Surfing the Web

SURF TOPICS

www.surfline.com
This site has over 50 updated surf reports including a report for LBI, Belmar, Manasquan, and Cape May; along with weather conditions and tide tables. There are 15 live video cams featuring the East and West Coasts, Hawaii, and Costa Rica. If you don't trust your friends to give you a call when the surf is firing, you can also sign up for Surfline's "Surf Alert" that will send you an e-mail with the details.

www.surfingmuseum.org
Website for the International Surfing Museum: sports history, legends, music, and films

www.surftrader.com
This is a global website dedicated to surfing buying, selling, and research needs. Go to Surf Trader Interchange to look at or submit classified ads for FREE. (These ads can be enhanced for a nominal fee—$5-8). You can also research surf travel, read about auctions & events, submit FREE messages, or list a stolen board.

www.wetsand.com
This is a search engine and resource site dedicated to surfing. There are categorized sites for: lifestyle, travel, gear, surf sites, forecast, environment, culture (history, art, photography), waterman (wave ski, surf kayak, surf lifesaving, windsurf).

http://molasar.blackmagic.com/ses/surf/papers/home.html
This site is HUGE!!! It is the official U.S. Surfing Federation's information resource with the world's leading online library for surfing related papers. You'll find topics ranging from a thesis on surfboard hydrodynamics to articles about surfing legends. There is product research, medical information, "how to" articles, just to name a few categories.

SURFING ORGANIZATIONS

www.newjerseysurfco.com/aso
Website for **Atlantic Surfers' Organization** Nonprofit organization created to provide continuing education to surfers of all ages. ASO sponsors annual college scholarships; ocean-education/surf etiquette/safety programs; activities & social events. (Website maintained through the assistance of NJS)

www.christiansurfers.com
Website for **Christian Surfers United States**

www.njsc.org
Website for Long Beach Island-based **N.J. Surf Club**

www.surfrider.org
Website for **Surfrider Foundation** Nonprofit organization dedicated to protecting our oceans, waves, and beaches

www.damoon.net/sea/index2.html Website for **Surfer's Environmental Alliance (SEA)** Nationwide environmental group with surfing roots and causes in mind

LONG BEACH ISLAND

http://gis.dl.stevens-tech.edu/cgi-bin/cmn2.pl
Coastal monitoring network at LBI as brought to you directly by

Stevens Institute of Technology. This site provides live footage from the observation area on the 6800 block of Ocean Avenue in Brant Beach. There are updates every 10 minutes and information about wind speed and direction, water and air temperature

www.LBInet.com
Tide table & weather, maps & directions, events calendar, advertisers, free chat line

www.discoversouthernocean.org
Official website of the **Chamber of Commerce** (located on the Causeway in Ship Bottom). You'll have the opportunity to investigate: places to stay, places to eat, fun things to do, calendar of events, real estate offices, driving directions

www.longbeachisland.com (This one has everything)
—Boating & fishing guide, calendar of events, news, accommodations, restaurants, worship services, business & professional address book, and driving directions-Webcam sites of: Barnegat Bay from Egg Harbor Marina in Beach Haven Gardens; Little Egg Harbor from Bayview Park, Brant Beach; Atlantic Ocean from 68th Street Observation Deck, Brant Beach; and 12 other sites in coastal towns like—Atlantic City, Belmar, Cape May

ENVIRONMENT

"If you're not part of the solution,
you're part of the problem"

www.livingocean.org
Official website for **Alliance for a Living Ocean**
Includes events, featured articles, environmental alerts, legislative updates, "Kids Ask Aloysius" environmental questions, gift shop and membership information

www.cleanoceanaction.org
Official website for **Clean Ocean Action**
This group is dedicated to improving the water quality off the New Jersey/New York coast through research, citizen action, and public education. Website includes events, issues and education

www.mmsc.org
Official website for the **Marine Mammal Stranding Center**
Information about the center located in Brigantine, marine mammal information, how to report a stranding or become a local volunteer

www.saveourenvironment.org
Official website for the **Save Our Environment Action Center.** *Please give this one a look !!!* It gives you up-to-date news and reports on the most urgent environmental campaigns in a clear and concise way. Information is provided regarding who you can contact to voice your opinion. You can either write your own letter or one is already written that will be initialized with your information and then sent with the touch of a button. It was never so easy and quick to make a BIG difference. From arsenic standards to the Arctic National Wildlife Refuge, when 75,000 people band together, people start to listen. Please don't let the opportunity go by to make a big difference, and while you're at it, tell a friend.

WEATHER

www.thecoolroom.org
This is a public service website maintained by the **Rutgers University Coastal Observation Lab—Institute of Marine and Coastal Services.** You can click on specific information for either fishermen, boaters, or swimmers/surfers/divers to find: *upwelling index* (predicts cold water) and *upwelling forecast coastal weather*—temperature, wind speed & direction, humidity & barometric readings from Tuckerton, Avalon, Atlantic City, and

Brant Beach s*ea surface temperatures* from satellite w*ave heights & periods* from selected New Jersey beaches—Brigantine and Brant Beach

www.fnoc.navy.mil/
This is unclassified public access to the **Numerical Meteorology & Oceanography Center.** All of the information is highly technical, including satellite imagery and lots of tables for information that is broken down into meteorology, oceanography, and climatology. If you can figure it out, it's helpful for long range forecasting or determining what the surf or weather may be in other parts of the world.

www.wannasurf.com
If you don't have a degree in meteorology or oceanography, this one is a little easier to understand and still gives you global information. There is swell & wind information from NOAA sources to help with a seventy-two hour forecast and swell size & direction from the U.S. Navy data to help make a five day prediction. The site also gives you a message board, info on surf spots, and surf news.

Why We Surf

Name: Jack Bushko   **Age:** 46   **Years Surfing LBI:** 28
Hometown: Langhorne, PA (Surfed Seaside years before finding LBI)
Occupation: Windsurfing Instructor (Island Surf and Sail—Brant Beach)

Other Places Surfed: Florida, North Carolina, Rhode Island

Favorite LBI Surfing Moment: Barnegat Light shoals, Summer 1996—Huge and perfect; Surfing with my son Josh. I built Josh his first board when he was five years old. He became a really good surfer and has surfed well in ESA and NSSA contests. He was also captain of the Southern Regional High School Surf Team. Watching him grow up and be a part of all that has been wonderful.

Why I Surf: Fun . . . Good exercise . . . Grew up doing it . . . Escape reality . . . A way to enjoy the beautiful planet that we have.

Jack is very accomplished in the windsurfing arena. He has written articles for a number of years for *Windsurfing* magazine and *New England Windsurfing Journal*. He is also skilled in off-shoots of the sport such as kitesailing and icesailing. Jack has been "windsurfing on ice" for twenty-five years. He has also developed and manufactured equipment for the sport through the company Free Skate. Is it just as hard to pass up a day of good ice as it is to pass up a day of good waves? According to

Jack, it's harder, because "good ice is so rare in these parts." The winter of 2002-2003 had some of the most consistently cold days in recent record. The result was ice in the bay that was three to four inches thick. Jack couldn't pass it up, even though he was recovering from Achilles tendon surgery. He was out on the ice even with a cast on. (Do not try this at home.) Jack describes an incredible adrenalin rush because of the tremendous speed and the realization that you are on frozen water.

Jack deserves credit for being a tremendous water sports supporter. He has organized the Annual Harvey Cedars Paddleboard Race for five years and counting. He has also helped organize surfing, windsurfing, and beach volleyball competitions. When not in the water themselves, Jack and his son, Josh Bushko, are out capturing the whole gamut of LBI water activities on film. They pride themselves in gladly giving exposure to some of the less visible water sports. Their programs, "Wet and Wild" and "Beach Bums" have aired regularly in the summer on the local cable station. Look forward to seeing "Beach Bums" this summer with new underwater footage. Josh, will be manning that camera and working toward his dream of becoming an accomplished water videographer.

* * *

Name: Rev. Chris Comfort   **Age:** 40   **Years Surfing LBI:** 35
Hometown: Manahawkin
Occupation: Minister (Bayside Chapel—Barnegat, NJ)

Other Places Surfed: Hawaii, Barbados, Costa Rica, Mexico, Dominican Republic, California, Up & Down the East Coast
Favorite LBI Surfing Moment: I think my favorite surfing moments are when I'm out with my family surfing 7-11 Beach in Ship Bottom. I have the most fun just watching my kids enjoy riding waves.

Why I Surf: If I didn't surf all these beautiful waves that God created, they would go to waste.

I thank God for LBI and for all the entertainment that it has brought to me and my family.

* * *

Name: Jesse Frack   **Age:** 48   **Years Surfing LBI:** 36
Hometown: Barnegat
Occupation: Musician, Dry wall taper—artistic taping (special curves & angles), pristine jobs only—no sloppy fast jobs taken

Other Places Surfed: Hawaii, California, Mexico, Florida, North Carolina

Favorite LBI Surfing Moment: Harvey Cedars

Why I Surf: It's an expression of freedom

Mary Frack, Jesse's wife, (Check out the article about her in the chapter—"Ladies of LBI") had this to say: "Jesse took up surfing with the locals when he moved to LBI from Paramus when he was twelve years old. He was hooked immediately. He would paddle out at 7A.M., come in around 12 Noon, jam down two hamburgers and paddle out for another five hour session! We met at the Hudson House in 1973 and made a surf connection for life. He always put waves at the top of his priority list, keeping him from work, family, and even food . . . all with my blessings, because I understand the need for good waves. Jesse could have four hours in before I even got to the beach with three little kids. I was satisfied with a couple one hour sessions. We are lucky to have the same love. I saw Jesse for the first time when I was fifteen years old. I later realized that it was he who had dropped in, sideslipped, spun backwards, got tubed, and came flying out to the delight of a Holgate surfing contest crowd."

How's that for love? Not only does Mary let Jesse surf when he wants to, but she even filled out this survey for him.

* * *

Name: Ken Gallant   **Age:** 49   **Years Surfing LBI:** 34
Hometown: Beach Haven Park
Occupation: Gallant Marketing

Other Places Surfed: All East Coast, California, Mexico, El Salvador, Costa Rica, Hawaii, Australia, France, Caribbean,

Favorite LBI Surfing Moment: The day they invented wax . . . before that it was a pretty slippery sport.

Why I Surf: Surfing is a fun sport, and so is bowling, but who takes exotic bowling trips to the South Pacific.

* * *

Name: Albert Gomez   **Age:** 47   **Years Surfing LBI:** 27
Hometown: Beach Haven (born in Germany)
Occupation: Craft Gallery Owner & Potter—
Crafts at the Marketplace—Schooner's Wharf, Beach Haven

Other Places Surfed: North Shore Kauai, Hawaii (every winter for 11 years); North Shore Maui, North Carolina, Florida, New York; Lake Michigan—Milwaukee, Wisconsin!! (I was a graduate student in fine arts in the winter of 1979. My board and wetsuit were with me just in case . . . There was a raging storm—big waves. It was great—it was *cold*).

Favorite LBI Surfing Moments: Like every surfer, I remember certain stand-out sessions on LBI. Surfing a July storm in the early 1970s with barrels bigger than a Beach Haven trash truck. Surfing five foot beach break with perfect barrels directly at a ten foot carve-out of the dune on 13th Street after a summer storm. About twenty years ago, the National Guard was evacuating the island during a big fall storm. Three buddies and I took a boat through two foot chop across the bay and beached it in Ship Bottom. As we were carrying our boards up the street, armed Guardsmen tried to intercept us. They chased us for a while but we dodged around and ran for the surf. That day we surfed twelve foot faces, all by ourselves, for three or four hours. When we got out, the Guard was gone. All surfers remember their epic days—the triumphant successes and the scary wipe-outs. But for me, my favorite LBI surfing moments are when Holyoke is breaking too big for the crowds and all the local boys are out. That's when I feel at home.

Why I Surf: Surfing is a personal journey for me—never a competition. I surf because I can't imagine not surfing—for the waves, yes, and all the good times in the water with different friends, in different places, at different times—it lights up my life.

* * *

Name: Rev. Dr. Larry Hand **Age:** 46 **Years Surfing LBI:** 33
Hometown: Reading, PA
Occupation: Lutheran Minister, Assistant to the Bishop SEPA Synod ELCA, Marriage and Family Counselor

Other Places Surfed: Rhode Island, South Carolina, Florida, Hawaii

Favorite LBI Surfing Moment: Summer 2001, surfing the "Boneyard" with my friend Billy Handy in shoulder high perfection in thick fog! You could only see the wave you were riding but we could hear each other hoot with pleasure as we rode on one perfect wave after another! A very ethereal moment! (I had to look up ethereal myself . . . It means unearthly, otherworldly, etc.). Hurricane Olga 2001 . . . Smelling the wood smoke being carried to the lineup by gentle offshore winds on a perfect November day . . . a little chill in the air . . . water temperature still in the sixties . . . surf chest-to-head high from a peeling hurricane ground swell.

Why I Surf: Surfing isn't just something to do, it is a style of living. For me, I feel most alive when I'm in the water . . . spiritually, emotionally, physically! A soulful awakening; a "baptismal" type cleansing that brings me closer to the Creator and to myself as part of creation when I'm in the ocean. Surfing is also a humbling experience. There are times when everything is going well—you've got the groove going—and other times when the ocean kicks my ass . . . we all need those moments to help us understand that life isn't just about us. It's about the God who makes the waves and entrusted us with the gift of life in which to enjoy them. Surfing keeps me in touch with that and reminds me that we are a small but significant part of something vast and universal!

"In the beginning God created the heavens and the earth . . . and the Spirit of God was moving over the face of the waters. And God said, "Let there be light!" (Genesis 1:2 & 4) Most people don't realize that God, *"moving across the face of the waters,"* not the Hawaiians, was the first to surf. It was a dawn patrol, no less, in the light of the first sunrise ever! If God surfed from the beginning of creation, then it must be something special! I find myself wondering what the conditions were during that primordial first session ever! Furthermore, if we have been created in God's image, then it would follow that we who live to surf, and surf to live, have an inside track on living in the image of God! It's like having the perfect line on a perfect wave on a perfect day!

When the Bishop I serve wants to know why I missed a staff meeting for a September hurricane swell, I simply explain that "I was living in the image of God." It's hard for him to refute. Surfing also keeps me in touch with a wonderful community of friends that share the passion for this lifestyle. The common denominator of surfing allows people from all walks of life to stand on a common ground and share something special and unique. When you understand the stoke, and share the stoke with others, all titles and labels are washed away. You can be who you are with those around you, while you experience the fullness of life. Surfing is truly one of the most soulful communal experiences on earth!

* * *

Name: Steve Jones   **Age:** 50   **Years Surfing LBI:** 40
Hometown: Surf City
Occupation: Painter—Steve Jones Painting Company

Other Places Surfed: Hawaii, Nova Scotia, Barbados to El Salvador. I like Mexico best—low crowds and good waves; Honestly, I really like surfing New Jersey on LBI. Even if it gets crowded, there's enough beach that you can always spread out.

Memorable LBI Surfing Moment: Surfing in Harvey Cedars on September, 11, 2001. The wind was offshore that day. I remember seeing smoke and thinking something was burning in Monmouth County, not realizing it was the Twin Towers.

Why I Surf: Surfing becomes your lifestyle. I can't imagine "not surfing." I'll just ride a longer and longer board until the day I die. At first surfing was more of a sport for me. As I moved into my thirties, the camaraderie and friendships were more important. Whether with friends or family, I've never taken a vacation that didn't revolve around surfing. My wife has never seen the Grand Canyon. She brought it up once and I wondered why she would even consider a vacation without the ocean. As I get older, I enjoy teaching and spending time with the younger generations. Surfing with my son became important.

* * *

Name: David Kaltenbach   **Age:** 50   **Years Surfing LBI:** 38
I started surfing on my older brother's 9'8" Duke Kahanamoku. It was so big and heavy I had to drag it on the pavement to get it to the beach. Consequently, he was always beating me up and we were forever doing ding repairs.
Hometown: Union, New Jersey—I had pictures of surfers

plastered on all my walls as a kid. I remember balancing my surfboard between the bed and my desk and practicing walking up and down the board. I moved to LBI in 1972 in order to surf year-round.

Occupation: Graphic artist—DK Designs specializing in commercial signs and lettering

Film producer/director/writer - Kaltenbach Productions: *kaltpro@earthlink.net*

Currently enrolled in the director's film program at New York University

Other Places Surfed: Barbados, Mexico, Hawaii, Central America, England

Why I Surf: Surfing is a great excuse for adventure in the world's playground. You have to be willing to sacrifice in order to travel, but it is well worth it. The surfers on LBI definitely travel.

David originally studied Marine Biology at Stockton in order to be close to the water and the surf. He eventually found that being self-employed as an artist gave him the best opportunity for surfing. He says he never had too much money back then, but spent what he had to stay in chattel houses (shacks) in Barbados for twenty to forty dollars a month or haciendas in Mexico which were two dollars a day with maid service. His surf trip to Costa Rica in 1988 with Jim Fitz-Randolph was a turning-point in his career. During that trip he was frustrated that he didn't have a movie camera to capture the howler monkeys they encountered close-up. His next trip to Barbados began his passion for "storytelling through film." Look for his film during Summer 2003: *Tales of a AquaNut*. It will feature surf and travel stories about Barbados, Mexico, LBI, Costa Rica, Tobago, and England. He is also working on a feature movie for Fall 2003: *Bridge to Nowhere*. For this project, he wrote the story and co-wrote the screenplay. David is no stranger to film production. He has produced several infomercials as well as a cable access program: *LBI Live.*

The thirty minute segments of *LBI Live* aired from 1994 to 1998 with what David described as a combination of wacky and whimsical skits interspersed with surfing footage and sponsor air time.

* * *

Name: Joseph Kaszas   **Age:** 49   **Years Surfing LBI:** 37
Hometown: Brant Beach
Occupation: Owner—Wida's Hotel & Restaurant in Brant Beach

Other Places Surfed: Florida

Favorite LBI Surfing Moment: Very hard to pick a favorite—I love it every time I go!
Why I Surf: I just enjoy being on the water—the beauty of it—the power of it—the ever-changing face of it.

* * *

Name: Ray Laird   **Age:** 45   **Years Surfing LBI:** 33
Hometown: I lived in Florida but spent every summer on LBI until high school. That's when I became a year-round LBI resident. My parents owned "Bakery Village Pantry" in Haven Beach. (Today it's the site of Honey Bubbles). I moved to Ocean City, New Jersey two years ago. It feels pretty strange being away from LBI. At least on LBI, I knew that someone would eventually recognize me and pick me up if I was on the side of the road.
Occupation: Youth Pastor—Cornerstone Ministries in Ocean City, New Jersey (Prior to that, many of you may remember Ray from his screen printing business - The Starving Artist in Brant Beach.)

Other Places Surfed: North Carolina, Florida, and New Hampshire for a surf contest that I went to with the Freedom Surf Team.

Favorite LBI Surfing Moment: I can still remember strategically parking cars when we knew we were in for a good southerly drift. We'd start at the "Cop Shop" (68th Street, Brant Beach) and end up somewhere down in Beach Haven.

Why I Surf: I never did much with team sports, but I really liked challenging myself with surfing. You couldn't rely on anyone else. The harder you practiced the better you got and the more fun you had.

Jack Poling can vouch for the fact that Ray helped his parents make donuts. He remembers being able to *smell* Ray paddling out to the line-up for dawn patrol. The Polings captured some of Ray's surfing in the "Coffee House" segment of: *LBI Saltwater High* (videocassette).

* * *

Name: Jonathan Law   **Age:** 42   **Years Surfing LBI:** 28
Hometown: Manahawkin (1970 to 1990—Holgate to Barnegat Light)
Occupation: Artist & Fine Framer of Pictures and Objects
Jonathan Law Fine Art Framing—1900 Long Beach Blvd., Surf City

Other Places Surfed: U.S. & British Virgin Islands

Favorite LBI Surfing Moment: In twenty-eight years, I've seen some amazing conditions up and down LBI's coast. The tropicals and low pressure storms, not the hurricanes, have produced my favorite swell conditions—well-overhead, usually ridable, and with warm water. Call a few friends, pick a good spot, and surf all day.

Why I Surf: Being raised in North Jersey (West Field), moving to

LBI in 1974, I was already versed in sports of all kinds. Surfing and skateboarding gained my interest. It didn't take me long to get the hang of it. However, to my amazement, the all natural emotion overwhelmed me with stoke. No matter how big or what the weather, any day is an experience. Now with my daughter learning the sport and also surfing with my nephew, the next generation will learn to love what we see and feel.

* * *

Name: Josh Law   **Age:** 15   **Years Surfing LBI:** 8
Hometown: Beach Haven
Other Places Surfed: Up & Down the East Coast, Hawaii

Favorite LBI Surfing Moment: Pretty much every time I go out. But, if I had to pick a favorite, it would be the first time I got barreled. My dad and my brother saw the whole thing.

Why I Surf: Originally, I started surfing because my dad and brother did. Then it became something much more. It's like an addiction. If I don't surf a day, (regardless of the conditions—I surf everyday), I feel I didn't accomplish anything that day. Surfing is my self-expression and my stress-release. It's a way for me to be Josh Law.

Josh surfs on the Southern Regional High School Surf Team and is consistently one of their top three competitors. Josh also competes in ESA events. He placed first in his very first surfing contest, and several times since then. He's LBI talent you'll want to keep an eye on.

* * *

Name: Bob Muroff   **Age:** 63   **Years Surfing LBI:** 40
Hometown: Long Beach Township & Beach Haven
Occupation: Long Beach Island Trailer Park—Owner & Manager

Other Places Surfed: Oahu, Maui, Australia, Cabo San Lucas, California, Montauk-Long Island, Puerto Rico, British Virgin Islands, Bahamas, Israel

Favorite Surfing Moments: Too many to note, however: First trip to Hawaii; Surfing a challenging day at Makaha in the early 1960s; Surfing the large epic day at Ditch Plains-Montauk Point on September 11, 2001.

Why I Surf: I surf for the wonderful joy of it. It is very definitely "a way of life." It keeps me physically and mentally fit. It is a strong and happy sport, an art form. It connects to "well-being" and spiritual feelings for lack of a better word. It connects to our deepest roots—sea, sky, & sun.

> *Surfing is about "doing it,"*
> *not talking about it,*
> *and about "surfing for life,"*
> *and about good surfing friends.*
> *It's about teaching,*
> *and helping others,*
> *to learn*
> *and love surfing.*

What Bob didn't tell you, is that he placed third in the Grand Master's Division (50+) at the Halloween Pro-Am held in San Clemente, California in 1992. Hosted by the Professional Longboarding Association, the Pro Final featured legends like: Joel Tudor, Joey Hawkins, Herbie Fletcher, and David Nuuhiwa. To further appreciate Bob's great athleticism, four years ago this regular-foot taught himself to take-off; I repeat, take off, not just ride, goofy-foot. That's pretty good for any age. Bob is very excited to do whatever he can to preserve and promote the sport of surfing. LBI couldn't have a better surfing ambassador. Bob is the stuff that surfing legends are made of.

* * *

Name: Bob Nugent   **Age:** 50   **Years Surfing LBI:** 37
Hometown: Brant Beach
Occupation: Self-employed Restaurant Owner—Ship Bottom Shellfish, Mud City Crab House, & Baja Grill

Other Places Surfed: All of East Coast, California (10x), El Salvador (2x), India, Fiji (2x), Mexico (5x), Barbados (15x), Hawaii (18x) Australia (2x), New Zealand (2x), Costa Rica, Puerto Rico (4x), Ireland

Favorite LBI Surfing Moment: Too many barrels in the fall & winter to pick just one

Why I Surf: Everything in nature has a balance, and so should our lives. Surfing is a great example of how natural balance works. When a surfer rides a wave, his or her positioning has to be just right. It's your position on the board, not just your own innate balance which enables the miracle of wave riding. The same is true in my life and my family's life. We own and operate three successful restaurants and still find time to surf and play in the ocean. If you look closer, it's by no accident that we carved out this lifestyle. Sure, I've missed some great surfing days because of the business, but, as it turns out, after thirty-seven years I'm still surfing year-round. Many of my friends have long since quit. I get to surf anytime, anywhere in the world, except June through September when we're working 24/7. Because I feel in balance with family, work, and ocean, I am a happy man.

* * *

Name: Joe Piscopo
Years Surfing LBI: I've been surfing over thirty-five years! I started when I was about thirteen years old. Not that I'm very good. The best there's been on LBI: Chucky Barfoot. So smooth with a

longboard, could make it do anything. You could have as much fun surfing a wave as you could watching him.

Hometown: I was born in Passaic, brought up in Essex County, live in Hunterdon County, but my sentimental home is definitely Long Beach Island!

Occupation: Comedian (Does *Saturday Night Live* sound familiar?)

Favorite LBI Surfing Moment: When it's early morning, the sun is kicking off the water from "the outside," the waves are Jersey glass—maybe 4' breaking right—soft offshore wind—and I'm with my son and friends I've known a lifetime. It doesn't get much better than that. My favorite LBI surfing moment is every time I'm out there. I remember surfing Holgate all day . . . Our moms would drive us down there, boards sticking out of the trunk of the family car.

Other Places Surfed: New York, Florida, and Hawaii. Makaha on Oahu has some of the best waves I've ever seen. After almost getting in trouble with a local for unintentionally cutting him off . . . and as all the locals were watching me as they were paddling out, I finally got my own wave . . . a screaming six foot wall, shoulder all to myself . . . I took off right at the lip and promptly wiped out on my face. I haven't been back since. Also in Hawaii, I had the 'honor' of surfing the inside break at Waimea Bay. Just me and two other guys . . ."Hey," they said, "You're Joe Piscopo, right?" Unfortunately, I said "Yes," because on the next wave, a twelve foot monster, with roaring white water, I took the drop down the face, right on my ass. It was good to get back to Jersey.

* * *

Name: Jack Ryan **Age:** 45 **Years Surfing LBI:** 33
Hometown: West Creek
Occupation: Lawyer
Other Places Surfed: Hawaii, Mexico, California, Rhode Island, New York, North Carolina, Florida, Tortola, Bermuda

Favorite Surfing Moment: When it's consistent and everybody is getting waves.

Why I Surf: I have to.

Jack Ryan was the legal representative for the Surfrider Foundation—New Jersey Chapter, when the "Holyoke Avenue Groin Modification Project" was under consideration by the Army Corp of Engineers (See "Holyoke Avenue Surfers Alliance" chapter for more details). Jack says that he learned a lot about activism from Albert Gomez and Betsy Wurzburg, who worked tirelessly gathering and organizing the scientific data as well as strategizing.

Jack was also ready to get his feet wet when Harvey Cedars considered shutting down the Hudson Avenue surfing beach. Jack works closely with Phil Mylod, an attorney for the New Jersey chapter. Together, they decide if a concern is a Surfrider issue, and then use grassroots organizing to "deal with local problems locally."

* * *

Name: Tice Ryan   **Age:** 48   **Years Surfing LBI:** 36
Hometown: Pittsburgh, PA (Possibly the best surfer ever from Pittsburgh)*
Occupation: Long Beach Township Beach Patrol—Training Director

Other Places Surfed: Hawaii, California, Costa Rico, Puerto Rico, Dominican Republic, Tortola, Barbados, Mexico, Florida, North Carolina, New York,

Favorite LBI Surfing Moments: Surfing my 9'6" slug on big days; Finishing third in Holyoke contest (highest placing regular foot); Winter surfing 2001-02.

Why I Surf: After all these years, it's still the coolest thing to do. Also, the girls love it that I can still rip, tear, and lacerate at my age. It's great to see more women out there ripping!

We hated to break Tice the news that East Coast Surfing Legend, Murph the Surf, was also from Pittsburgh. That's okay, we have it on very good authority that Tice runs a very close second.

* * *

Name: Bob Selfridge   **Age:** 39   **Years Surfing LBI:** 25
Hometown: Ship Bottom, Harvey Cedars (SRHS Class of 1982)
Occupation: Sixth Grade Teacher—LBI School, Lifeguard in the summers—Barnegat Light for twenty-three years

Other Places Surfed: Up & Down the East Coast, California, Mexico, Puerto Rico, Indonesia

Favorite LBI Surfing Moments: Being able to surf with my kids . . . I had my daughter out on a surfboard with me for the first time when she was six months old. My son rode his first wave this past summer at four years old.

Surfing for me personally . . . Barnegat Light shoals, after Hurricane Bob, a half mile off the inlet. Those were the biggest waves I've ever seen on LBI.

Why I Surf: That's easy . . . I'm addicted.

According to at least one source, Bob may be one of the best all-around watermen on the island. When he's not pushing himself out in the water, he's helping to promote water sports. He has been instrumental in organizing everything from contests for windsurfing, longboarding, and volleyball, to an "Invitation Only" **Real** Surf Contest. This event, held in the late 80s, was only contested on the biggest surf days with the location subject to change based on the best spot for the day. (Hey Bob, I don't remember getting an invitation). Bob also brings his love for the sport into the classroom. "A lot of my students know that I surf. After class they'll sometimes ask me what I think the surf will be like. Now with the Internet, we get to sit down and look up information on the computer. I surf quite a bit in the morning, before the school day starts. They can usually tell if it's a morning that I've been out surfing. For one thing, I get into the classroom dripping wet. I also have a pretty mellow attitude the whole rest of the day." Anyone that's interested in getting surf lessons from a real "surfing teacher" can reach Bob at 361-2218.

* * *

Name: Dawson Smith **Age:** 51 **Years Surfing LBI:** 40
Hometown: Trenton, N.J.
Occupation: Owner—Lawn-Gevity Landscaping

Other Places Surfed: New Hampshire, Massachusetts, Rhode Island, Florida, California, Hawaii, El Salvador, Puerto Rico, Barbados

Favorite LBI Surfing Moments: Long, long rides across the bars . . . pre-jetties, early to mid-60s. Late 60s Holyoke . . . Take-offs way, way out in front of the jetty and rides for blocks. Prime Harvey Cedars 1970 to 1975. Years of just the crew, fifteen to twenty guys. We looked for years saying, "There are no young kids surfing . . . They're all out skateboarding and aren't old enough to drive." The summer of Hurricane Felix . . . The benchmark year for all the young surfers. My first "no-stroke" take-off in this my fortieth year of water brotherhood.

Why I Surf: I surf to keep myself lined up and trim with the wave of life. There is the "jazz" of just thinking about waxing up for the go out. The swirl of excitement knowing you can free up yourself from the pace of the race and enjoy a wave. The chance to talk story with my water brothers from all the places I shared great waves and laughs.

* * *

Name: Erik Svensen **Age:** 32 **Years Surfing LBI:** 20
Hometown: Brant Beach
Occupation: Structural Engineer

Other Places Surfed: Massachusetts, New Hampshire, New York, North Carolina, Florida, Costa Rica; I lived in California for a year and surfed San Diego to Steamers Lane.

Favorite LBI Surfing Moment: The Saturday after Hurricane Gloria hit LBI. The wind was offshore, warm water, and perfect waves all day.

Why I Surf: Learning to surf provided me an experience to something that is so inspirational. Surfing allows me to experience the power of nature and then to use that energy to generate speed along the surface of the wave. It allows me to forget about any stress and relax. Surfing is a great experience. It allows me to bring that feeling with me to every aspect of my life.

* * *

Name: Daniel Unger **Age:** 48 **Years Surfing LBI:** 6
Hometown: Boyertown, PA; Ship Bottom since 1998
Occupation: Athletic Trainer, Director of Sports Medicine at Villanova University 1978 to 1998; Long Beach Township Beach Patrol; Presently in Nursing School

Favorite LBI Surfing Moments: Being pile-driven while still laying on my 10'2" surfboard. The board and I bounced off the ocean floor—trust me, not an easy thing to do. The last thing I remember was my brother-in-law saying, "Dan, you're gonna die." When I came up in one piece he just shook his head and chuckled. I know better now to check the wave conditions myself before suiting up and going out.

Why I Surf: To spend time with my wife

* * *

Name: Caroline Unger   **Age:** 37   **Years Surfing LBI:** 25
Hometown: Delran, N.J., Ship Bottom since 1998
Occupation: Physical Therapist; Summer help on weekends at family business—Brighton Beach Surf Shop: retail, ding repair, surf lessons; Oh yeah, and I wrote this book

Other Places Surfed: Rhode Island, North Carolina, Florida, California

Favorite LBI Surfing Moment: I can't remember a time ever being in the ocean without having some type of a board to enjoy the waves. I used it all—styrofoam paddleboards, boogie boards and skimboards. One of the defining moments was when I was about five years old and my brother and I went down to the beach on Berkeley Street with my aunt. (My parents were too busy in the summer running Brant Beach Surf Shop to go with us). A big storm had just passed through and the lifeguards hadn't yet made it down to the beach. I convinced my aunt that it was safe for me to go out on my belly board, since the lifeguards would be back soon. The fog was incredibly thick. As I paddled out I was aware of a dozen or more surfers around me. I had never actually been in the water at the same time as "real surfers" so I was in my glory. As they paddled further and further out, I continued to follow as fast as my little arms would carry me. Suddenly the fog cleared enough to visualize an incredible outside break. It was the biggest, most beautiful wave I had ever seen. I suspect my eyes got wide and I know that I said out loud, "Whoa . . . I have to get out there." Just then I felt something tug at my leg. It was a Beach Haven lifeguard who smiled and said, "No you're not . . . turn around and head in." I did go in, sooner than I wanted, but not before experiencing the pure stoke of seeing and feeling a big ocean wave.

Why I Surf: It's the one activity that benefits my entire wellbeing—the emotional, spiritual, and physical. Some days surfing is the ultimate adrenalin rush. Some days sitting on a surfboard is the most relaxing place to be on the planet.

Other: Just for the record, my surfing is only mediocre. (In case you were wondering). I would ruin my credibility writing this book if I told you otherwise. For anyone who wants to start, though . . . you don't have to be great at it to love it. You can also be reasonably comfortable surfing on LBI all year-round . . . honest.

My competition days were brief for the University of Florida Surf Team, since it conflicted with my collegiate track and field schedule. It did get me to the beach when I didn't have a car. In water competition, I've since been more successful in kayak and surf ski races including Women's First Place on the East Coast in the Surf Ski—1995 (Hollywood, Florida).

I've also spent a lifetime involved in surfboard repair. I think as soon as I could use scissors (four years old?), I was helping my dad in the off-season, cut fiberglass patches for the ding repairs he was doing in our basement. (We didn't know about ventilation back then). I was eventually promoted to measuring the catalyst, "chopping" the glass, and stirring the combinations. Then came sanding—first by hand, and then, thank goodness, I was allowed to use a palm sander before I permanently sanded off all my fingerprints. I know how to lay up fins, put in foam blocks, and put two halves back together. It's the only thing handy I've ever been able to do.

* . * *

Name: Jackie Unger **Age:** 2 ½ **Years Surfing LBI:** to be determined
Hometown: Ship Bottom
Why I Surf: Didn't know that I had a choice.

* * *

Name: Bill Willem **Age:** 49 **Years Surfing LBI:** 36
Hometown: Surf City

Occupation: Commercial clammer (Sandy Hook); Prior to that, worked with father who owned Bill's Seafood in Surf City.

Other Places Surfed: Most of the East Coast and California. Spent many winters in Santa Barbara doing carpentry. Drove from LBI to El Salvador in 1975. That was a very interesting trip. There was one stretch of area in Mexico that according to the map looked to be about one hundred-fifty miles to get to the coast. It ended up taking thirteen hours. At one point we pulled off the side of the road to take a break and were shot at.

Why I Surf: There's nothing like riding a wave. There's tremendous self-satisfaction. It's hard to explain. It's something that only someone who surfs would really know. It removes you from everything. It heals you. It's always good.

Bill started surfing some local contests in Ocean City when he was fifteen years old. He later surfed on the Rick Surf Shop Team. Highly skilled riding both short and long boards, Bill has done very well in ESA events over the years. He has won the Northeast Region Senior Men's Longboard Competition twice. He even beat the legendary Peter Pan on his home surf in Rhode Island. Bill also made the finals in the East Coast Championship in 1999. Bill has passed on the surfing bug to sons Brendan (17) and Conner (11).

(**A**) Jack Ryan, Esquire (**B**) Tice Ryan, Beach Haven Crest (Surf Avenue), Easter 2000 (**C**) Bob Muroff, Beach Haven (Holyoke), October 2002 - 63 years young and looking as good as ever (**D**) Mary & Jesse Frack—Still making sweet music . . . and it all began while surfing on LBI (**E**) The Ungers—Daniel, Caroline, and Jackie, Fall 2002 (**F**) Eric Svensen, Brant Beach (40th Street), Hurricane Gordon 1994

Photo: Stacy

Photo: Grasso

(G) "Surfing Rev" Chris Comfort in need of some Divine intervention. (H) Joe Kaszas on a break from Wida's (I) That's Bob Nugent in the tube! Pipeline, 1976 (J) Ken Gallant getting "snaked" by Michael Lisiewski in North Beach Haven (13th Street), February 1999. (K) Al Gomez in the showroom of his Craft Gallery at Schooner's Wharf in Beach Haven. Every piece of pottery that he makes looks like the ocean. (L) Rev. Larry Hand at the North Shore 2002

Surfing Long Beach Island |203|

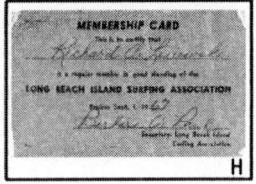

LBI SCRAPBOOK -THEN: (A) Mickey King, left, Dick Crosta and Gary Wenal after a Thanksgiving Day session on Centre Street in Beach Haven, circa 1966. **(B)** Picture that appeared in 1966 SRHS yearbook of Billy Hoffman's Woody. Pictured are: Chris Shultz (hood), Billy Hoffman (front door), Robert Stanton (behind back door), Dan Zwalley (back wheel). **(C)** Article that appeared in *The Sunday Bulletin (Philadelphia)*, July 12, 1964 crediting Rev. Dr. Earl Comfort, president of L.B.I.S.A. for his efforts. **(D)** Water decal circa 1967 **(E)** Picture of Bonnie Roth that appeared in *The Sunday Bulletin (Philadelphia)*, December 17, 1967. **(F)** "Party Wave" cartoon by *Hazel*, a.k.a. Bonnie Roth **(G)** Advertisement for surfing school that appeared in local papers in 1968 & 1969. **(H)** L.B.I.S.A. membership card

LBI SCRAPBOOK - NOW: (**A**) Tom Luker is still cracking the lip at 57 years old. This picture was taken in Puerto Rico, 2003. (**B**) Michael Lisiewski with a chilly ceiling overhead, North Beach Haven (13th Street), February 1999. (**C**) Bill Cain, exploding down the line in Beach Haven Terrace (Pennsylvania Avenue) after Hurricane Hortense, September 1996. (**D**) "Raising Cain" - Daniel Cain, pictured at 9-years-old. He's a "chip off the ol' block." (**E**) Jason Murray on a business trip in Indonesia, Summer 2000.

ISLAND LIVIN': (**Top**) Bill Handy paddling with the dolphins * A seasonal message from Bob Nugent at Ship Bottom Shellfish (**Bottom**) Commercial fishing boats on a winter day in Barnegat Light * My daughter Jackie when she was twelve months old - I think she's a natural * Aerial shot of LBI

Acknowledgements

COVER PHOTO

Top—Dawn Patrol with Michael Lisiewski, Bill Simon and Andy Taam Photo: Stacy Lisiewski
Bottom Left—Michael Lisiewski at Wooden Jetty Photo: Stacy Lisiewski
Bottom Right—Justin Citta Photo: Ray Hallgreen

"Mahalo nui loa," That's Hawaiian for "Thank you very much"

First and foremost, I need to thank my brother **Michael Lisiewski** who helped me extensively with his time and equipment doing all the photo scanning, graphic design, and lay-outs for the inside and also the wonderful cover. I couldn't have completed this project without him.

He's snaked every good wave I've ever had and also pulled a prank or two. Pulling the wetsuit zipper down and then pushing me into 50° water immediately comes to mind. Nevertheless, he's always been there when I've needed him. Some of the best times I've ever had have been in the water next to him.

My sincerest thanks to these other fine people who went "above and beyond" to make this a reality:

Steve "Kahuna" Scarano for sharing all you know about surfing history.

Tice Ryan for hooking me up through the vast network of people that you know.

Anne Bungo for your wonderful editing skills. (I know it took a really long time).

Also **Mary Gruber, Bob Stanton** and **Jay Mann** for your footwork

Special thanks to **God**

The photos were a large part of this project. Several professional photographs appear throughout the book. My deepest thanks to:

Robert Garrabrant for his picture of Tice Ryan. Rob has surfed off 78th Street for thirty years. His great shot was taken with a digital camera and 10x zoom.

Ray Hallgreen for his shot of Justin Citta on the cover and also in the chapter: "SRHS Surf Team." Ray is a Trenton native who started surfing when he was sixteen years old (1966). That was the year that his parents rented a summer home on LBI. Stoked on the surfing experience, he vowed to never again live too far from the beach. He now resides in Seaside Park and works as an engineer for the N.J. D.O.T. He has been taking surfing pictures since the 1970's and is presently a senior photographer for *Eastern Surf* magazine and a contributing photographer for *Surfer* magazine. Ray usually shoots from the beach with a 600mm lens. He also takes water shots with a 35mm camera in a fiberglass housing, relying on a set of Churchill fins to get him out in the line-up.

James F. Joiner and **Edward W. Greevy, III,** Publishers of *Competition Surf* whose pictures appear in "Koseff's Surf Shop" and "Sixties Surfing Contests." They allowed us to reproduce multiple shots from the article "Surf City: LBI Surfing Championships" which appeared in their Spring 1966 edition. *Competition Surf* was an East Coast contest-oriented magazine in 1966 and 1967, distributed by Hearst Corporation out of New York.

Heather Lewis, Marketing Director of Ron Jon Surf Shop for coordinating use of photos of Jamie DeWitt and Ron Jon Surf Shop—past and present.

Robert Mignona, Publisher of *Surfing Magazine* for allowing reproduction of photos that appeared in *International Surfing:* "Long Beach Island on the Atlantic," June 1965, Photos by Francis Laping "The Dynamic Duo: Puerto Rico's Crashboat and Gas Chamber," Annual 1969, Photos by Roger Bakst

Chris Pfeil, a "household name" around these parts for his great surf photography and also being an all-around nice guy. He graciously donated multiple shots included in: "Introduction to LBI," "LBI Surfer," "SRHS Surf Team," "Local Breaks."

Clark & Jack Poling of Poling Productions. The great shots in the chapter: "Poling Productions" were 'grabbed' from the 1989 videocassette production: *LBI SaltwaterHigh*

My thanks to: **Margaret "Pooch" Buchholz,** (Managing Editor, *The Beachcomber*) for allowing reproduction of the quotations from Stretch Pohl that were preserved for us in *The Beachcomber*, 1969.

My thanks to the following individuals for the use of photos from personal collections:

Ric Anastasi	Jason Murray
Chuck Barfoot	Chill Paul
Amy Cain	Irene Pohl
Rev. Earl Comfort	John Ryan
Barbara Conover	Steve "Kahuna" Scarano
Dick Crosta	Robert Stanton
Michelle DeGennaro	Eric Svensen
Mary Frack	Margaret Walters
Michael Lisiewski	Carl "Tinker" West
Bonnie (Roth) Lauer	Tom Luker

Anyone who has young people in their home is probably familiar with the 2002 Walt Disney Pictures animated film: *Lilo and Stitch*. In this film, a creature from outer space experiences surfing in Hawaii. The following sentiment is repeated several times in the film:

> *"Ohana" means family.*
> *Family means no body gets left behind ...*
> *or forgotten.*

The Long Beach Island Surfing *Ohana* is a very special group of people. As Dave Kaltenbach pointed out to me, "LBI surfers are everywhere. I've bumped into them out in a jungle in Costa Rica, a line-up in Barbados and at Newark Airport as we both waited to embark on separate surfing trips."

I know that there are some people who I unintentionally "left behind" while preparing this manuscript. So that they won't be "forgotten" members of our family, please let me know who they are for future reference. I have tried very hard to verify the authenticity of all the information. If there is information that you think is incorrect, please let me know that as well. I look forward to hearing from you with your input. I can be reached through e-mail at: *ungerlbi@juno.com*

You can also find me in my favorite place of all - Out in the surf off LBI!

The beautiful native Hawaiian, Rell Sun, was a top women's competitor since the early 1970s. She finished as high as third in the 1982 world ratings and was one of the world's premier longboarders, almost up until her death in 1998 at the age of 46. She spread "aloha" around the world and was one of surfing's finest ambassadors. I leave you with her thoughts about surfing:

> *"The richest heritage you can have is a surfing heritage.*
> *We consume less and we travel more. We are the gypsies of*
> *the earth and people love our lifestyle."*
> (even if we are from "Joisy")

BVG